THE FOUNDATION AND APPLICATIONS OF MONOPOLISTIC COMPETITION

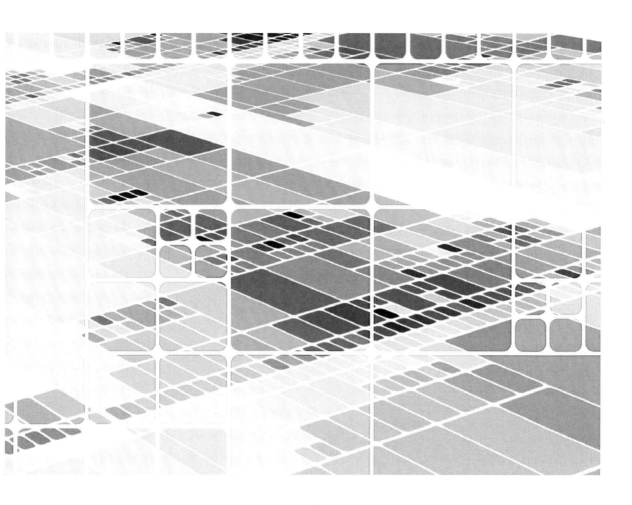

TOSHIHIRO ATSUMI

SANKEISHA

THE FOUNDATION AND APPLICATIONS OF MONOPOLISTIC COMPETITION

Copyright © 2018 TOSHIHIRO ATSUMI

SANKEISHA CO., LTD.

2-24-1 Chumaru-cho, Kita-ku, Nagoya, Aichi, JAPAN

ISBN: 978-4-86487-924-8 C3033 ¥1100E

Printed in Japan

Contents

Preface   i

Chapter 1   **The foundation of monopolistic competition in general equilibrium**   **1**

Chapter 2   **Inequality and non-strategic entry deterrence in monopolistic competition**   **9**

Chapter 3   **Making sense of the diffusion of mass production: a theoretical account of the rise of mass production**   **17**

Chapter 4   **Competition policy in a globalized world: how does a policy taken by one country work in a globalized world?**   **31**

Chapter 5   **Natural advantage and economic geography: when does a mining site develop into a city?**   **41**

Chapter 6   **Spatial organization of firms in a changing global economic environment: implications for Tokyo**   **51**

References   **69**

Preface

This book introduces various theoretical applications of the monopolistic competition model. By departing from the perfect competition framework, the monopolistic competition model captures the modern features of an economy that includes competition by firms producing differentiated goods with increasing returns to scale technology. The firms are not price-takers and have monopoly power over their products but face competition from other firms producing similar products. Consumers in the market have a love of variety and enjoy the variety of goods and services offered by the monopolistically competitive firms.

The structure of the book is as follows: Chapter 1 reviews the foundation of monopolistic competition in general equilibrium; Chapters 2 through 6 present original applications of monopolistic competition theory. The primary aim of these chapters is to demonstrate that the theory of monopolistic competition can be applied to a variety of issues and events, including not only current issues such as inequality and globalization but also historical epochs such as the early diffusion of mass production.

In Chapter 2, the entrepreneur specification of monopolistic competition is applied to the issue of inequality. It is shown that inequality between entrepreneurs and their employees can increase infinitely. Such inequality is eliminated when all are allowed to start their own businesses and there are no further profitable opportunities for new entry. The long-run share of entrepreneurs depends only on the consumer's love of variety. This share also serves as an upper-bound prediction of the share of entrepreneurs within the population. However, analysis of the same model also finds that the firms have incentives to deter new entry, which suggests that inequality can remain.

Chapter 3 describes the general equilibrium implications of technological change. Specifically, it offers a theoretical account of the rise of mass production. Despite being widely used and studied in a variety of disciplines, mass production has not been analyzed rigorously from an economic theory point of view. The analysis in this chapter is an attempt to fill that gap, in order to make sense of mass production. Defining mass production as a new system in which goods can be produced more cheaply but which requires higher fixed costs, the conditions under which the economy switches to mass production are derived by analyzing a general equilibrium monopolistic competition model with technology choice. It is found that once the transition to mass production takes place, there is no reversal to the old way of production unless preferences change. It is also shown that such a transition of the economy to mass production, driven by the decisions of profit-seeking firms to adopt new mass production technologies, always improves welfare. These findings may increase our understanding of some of the underlying forces that drove the diffusion of mass production in the twentieth century.

Chapter 4 examines the global impact of a competition policy adopted by one country. In particular, this chapter analyzes the consequence of entry regulation by one country in a world where goods are freely traded. It is shown that such a policy will not affect world welfare. Entry regulation reduces the mass of firms and varieties of goods supplied locally in the regulating country, but the existence of international trade induces the same mass of firm entry in other countries. The only change would be an asymmetry in the resulting industrial structure of the countries involved. The result illustrates one of the typical consequences of economic policies in today's globalized world.

Chapter 5 discusses natural advantage and economic geography, using mining sites as an illustration. Mining sites are special locations that allow the extraction of natural resources. Do such locations attract corporate activities leading to the creation of a city? Casual observation of geography tells us that some mining sites do, in fact, develop into cities. Examples include Johannesburg in South Africa, Kalgoorlie in Australia, and Magnitogorsk in Russia. However, not all mining sites become cities, which suggests that there exist certain conditions under which this development occurs. Accordingly, this chapter explores the question, when does a mining site become a mining city? Using ideas developed in the new economic geography literature, it is shown that there is a range of potential mining site locations that can develop into mining cities and that a mining site outside that range will remain just a mining site.

Chapter 6 analyzes a simple economic model of the spatial organization of monopolistically competitive firms, focusing on where they choose to locate their headquarters. It explains the coexistence of large firms with stand-alone metropolitan headquarters and smaller firms spatially integrated in other places. The model is extended to consider the link between a change in the global economic environment and a metropolitan area through the impact of the change on the spatial organization of firms. The results suggest that the current trends of international trade liberalization in the Asia-Pacific region and the shrinking of Japan's economy are likely to work as additional forces concentrating Japan's economic activities in Tokyo.

About the author

Toshihiro Atsumi is an Associate Professor in the Faculty of Economics at Meiji Gakuin University. He graduated from the Faculty of Economics at Hitotsubashi University in 1993 and later completed his master's course in the same department (1997). After working at the Mitsubishi Research Institute Inc. (1997-2005), he traveled to England where he earned his Ph.D. at the University of Nottingham (2009). After completing a research fellowship at the same university, he took up his present position in 2010. He specializes in international trade and applied microeconomic theory. His recent research concerns international trade and domestic industrial locations, international trade and cities, human migration, counterfeits, and automobile trade.

Acknowledgement

The author greatly appreciates the financial support of Grants-in-Aid for Scientific Research (16H06551) from the Japan Society for the Promotion of Science.

Chapter 1 The foundation of monopolistic competition in general equilibrium

1. Introduction

This chapter explains the workings of monopolistic competition in general equilibrium based on the model developed by Dixit and Stiglitz (1977). This general equilibrium version of monopolistic competition provides the basis for subsequent applications in Chapters 2 through 6. Assumptions regarding consumers and firms are presented in the next section. Their behaviors are derived in Sections 3 and 4. Equilibrium is shown in Section 5. The final section describes the advantages of general equilibrium modeling of monopolistic competition.

2. Assumptions

Consumer preference

There are two types of goods in the economy - differentiated goods, labeled as 'manufactured' goods, and homogeneous goods, labeled as 'agricultural' goods. All consumers are assumed to have the same preferences. These preferences are described by the following two-tier structure:

$$U = M^{\mu} A^{1-\mu} \quad (0 < \mu < 1) \tag{1a}$$

$$M = \left[\int_0^n m(i)^{\rho} \, di \right]^{\frac{1}{\rho}} (0 < \rho < 1) \tag{1b}$$

The upper tier (1a) is a Cobb-Douglas function of the consumption of an aggregate of manufactured varieties (M) and the (homogeneous) agricultural good (A). The second tier (1b) defines M as a constant elasticity of substitution (CES) function, where $m(i)$ is the consumption of each manufactured variety i. M is therefore a CES composite of the total mass of varieties, n. The elasticity of substitution between any manufactured varieties is $1/(1-\rho) \equiv \sigma \quad (\sigma > 1)$.

Production technology and market structure

A firm producing a particular manufactured variety requires a fixed number (α) of workers and β workers per unit output. The firm thus faces increasing returns to scale. Its total cost for producing a given amount, q^M, is then

$$c(q^M) = \alpha w + \beta w q^M, \tag{2}$$

where w is the wage of the workers. It is assumed that manufacturing is monopolistically competitive.

2   Chapter 1

On the other hand, agriculture is a constant returns to scale sector also using labor as a factor of production. A unit of workers produces a unit of agricultural goods. Therefore, the total cost of producing a given amount of agricultural goods (q^A) is

$$c(q^A) = wq^A . \tag{3}$$

Perfect competition is assumed in the agricultural sector. The assumptions of the two sectors are highlighted in Table 1.1.

Factor endowment

The total population consists of L workers who are also consumers.

Table 1.1: The two sectors

	Technology	Market structure	Product differentiation
Manufacturing	IRS	Monopolistic competition	Differentiated by firm
Agriculture	CRS	Perfect competition	Homogeneous

3. Consumer behavior

For a given income Y, a given price p^A for the agricultural good, and a given price $p(i)$ for each manufactured variety, the consumer's problem is to maximize her utility, subject to the budget constraint

$$\int_0^n p(i)m(i)di + p^A A = Y . \tag{4}$$

Since the preference for manufactured varieties and the agricultural good are separable, and the second tier is homothetic in $m(i)$, the problem can be solved in two steps.[i] The first step is to choose $m(i)$. The second step is to allocate the expenditure between M and A.

Step 1: Consumers should choose $m(i)$ to minimize the cost of consuming M. This implies minimizing expenditure

$$\int_0^n p(i)m(i)di$$

subject to

$$\left[\int_0^n m(i)^\rho \, di \right]^{\frac{1}{\rho}} = M . \tag{5}$$

The first-order condition of the problem is that the marginal rate of substitution between any two manufactured varieties i and j is equal to their price ratio:

$$\frac{m(i)^{\rho-1}}{m(j)^{\rho-1}} = \frac{p(i)}{p(j)}. \tag{6}$$

Substituting (6) into (5) produces the following expression, which is the compensated demand function for manufactured variety j:

$$m(j) = \frac{p(j)^{\frac{1}{\rho-1}}}{\left[\int_0^n p(i)^{\frac{\rho}{\rho-1}} di\right]^{\frac{1}{\rho}}} M. \tag{7}$$

The minimum expenditure to consume M is, therefore,

$$\int_0^n p(j)m(j)dj = \left[\int_0^n p(i)^{\frac{\rho}{\rho-1}} di\right]^{\frac{\rho-1}{\rho}} M. \tag{8}$$

The term

$$\left[\int_0^n p(i)^{\frac{\rho}{\rho-1}} di\right]^{\frac{\rho-1}{\rho}}$$

in (8) is called the price index, G:

$$G \equiv \left[\int_0^n p(i)^{\frac{\rho}{\rho-1}} di\right]^{\frac{\rho-1}{\rho}} = \left[\int_0^n p(i)^{1-\sigma} di\right]^{\frac{1}{1-\sigma}}. \tag{9}$$

Using G, (7) can be written simply as

$$m(j) = \left[\frac{p(j)}{G}\right]^{-\sigma} M. \tag{10}$$

Step 2: The second step in the solution of the consumer's problem is to allocate income between M and A; that is, to maximize the upper tier utility function (1a), subject to the budget constraint $GM + p^A A = Y$. The first-order conditions indicate that μY should be spent on the composite of manufactured varieties and that $(1-\mu)Y$ should be spent on the agricultural good. Therefore, the demand functions for manufactured variety j and the agricultural good, respectively, are

$$m(j) = p(j)^{-\sigma} G^{\sigma-1} \mu Y \tag{11}$$

and

$$A = \frac{(1-\mu)Y}{p^A}. \tag{12}$$

4 Chapter 1

The result in (11) is important. Demand for each differentiated variety, that is, demand for each manufacturing firm's product, depends not only on the price of the product and income but also on the overall price level of the manufactured goods, which is represented by price index G. Other things being equal, the higher the value of G, the greater the demand for the product. Also from (11), the price elasticity of demand

$$\left[dm(j)/dp(j) \right] \Big/ \left[m(j)/p(j) \right]$$

can be derived as

$$\sigma + \left[p(j)^{1-\sigma} (1-\sigma) \right] \Big/ \int_0^n p(j)^{1-\sigma} \, dj .$$

However, because $n \to \infty$ with a continuum of manufactured varieties, the second term approaches zero. Therefore, the price elasticity of demand is simply σ.

4. Firm behavior

In the manufacturing sector, because of the infinite number of potential varieties and increasing returns to scale at the firm level, each firm becomes a sole producer of each differentiated variety. The first-order condition of profit maximization is then the equalization of marginal revenue and marginal cost. Since the demand elasticity that each firm faces is σ, manufacturing firms will exhibit the following mark-up pricing behavior

$$p^M \left(1 - \frac{1}{\sigma} \right) = \beta w^M , \tag{13}$$

and the price index of the manufactured goods is

$$G = \left[n \left(p^M \right)^{1-\sigma} \right]^{\frac{1}{1-\sigma}} = n^{\frac{1}{1-\sigma}} p^M . \tag{14}$$

The price index given by (14) implies that, for given prices of each variety, the larger the mass of manufacturing firms, the lower the price index of manufactured goods. This, combined with the demand expression in (11), implies that an increased mass of firms toughens competition through lowering the price index and reducing demand for each firm. Taking advantage of the symmetry of the firms, i is hereinafter dropped, and we focus on a typical firm in the manufacturing sector.

5. Equilibrium

Equilibrium requires market clearing in all goods and factor markets, and zero profit of firms as a result of free entry.

Agricultural sector

Because perfect competition leads to marginal cost pricing in the agricultural sector, $p^A = w$. Choosing the agricultural good as the numeraire and setting the wage equal to 1, $p^A = w = 1$.

Manufacturing sector

In the manufacturing sector, zero profit due to free entry requires operating profits to equal fixed cost. That is,

$$p^M q^M - \beta w q^M = \alpha w . \tag{15}$$

Labor market

Since there are n firms in the manufacturing sector, each of which employs $\alpha + \beta q^M$ units of workers, and the agricultural sector employs $(1-\mu)Y$ workers, full employment requires that

$$(1-\mu)Y + n(\alpha + \beta q^M) = L . \tag{16}$$

Manufactured goods market

The market clearing conditions for a typical manufactured variety can be shown as

$$(p^M)^{-\sigma} G^{\sigma-1} \mu Y = q^M . \tag{17}$$

Substituting for p^M in (15) using (13) and rearranging terms produces a constant equilibrium manufacturing firm size:

$$q^M = \frac{\alpha(\sigma-1)}{\beta} . \tag{18}$$

Substituting (18) into (16) and rearranging terms results in an equilibrium manufacturing firm mass of

$$n = \frac{\mu L}{\alpha \sigma} , \tag{19}$$

and it can be confirmed that (18) and (19) satisfy (17).

In comparison to the perfectly competitive agricultural sector, where there are no significant firm characteristics, in the monopolistically competitive manufacturing sector, per firm size and firm mass are derived as an equilibrium outcome: Per firm size, as given by (18), depends on three exogenous parameters, α, β and σ. An increase in fixed costs (α) increases equilibrium firm size, while an increase in marginal input requirement (β) reduces firm size. An increase in the elasticity of substitution (σ) increases firm size as well. Firm mass, as given by (19), depends on four exogenous

6   Chapter 1

parameters, μ, L, α, and σ. An increase in the expenditure share of manufactured goods (μ) and/or an increase in population size (L) will increase equilibrium firm mass, n. On the other hand, an increase in fixed costs (α) and/or an increase in the elasticity of substitution (σ) will reduce n. Therefore, if consumers' love of variety is weak (that is, if consumers place little value on variety), then there will be less varieties (or firms) and these varieties will be produced in greater quantities.

Finally, the real wage (ω), or indirect utility, can be used to evaluate economic welfare:

$$\omega = \frac{w}{G^{\mu}\left(p^{A}\right)^{1-\mu}} = G^{-\mu} = \left(n^{\frac{1}{1-\sigma}}p^{M}\right)^{-\mu} = \left(\frac{\mu L}{\alpha\sigma}\right)^{\frac{\mu}{\sigma-1}}\left(\frac{\sigma-1}{\sigma\beta}\right)^{\mu}. \tag{20}$$

Table 1.2: Variables in the model

Exogenous		Endogenous	
μ	Expenditure share of manufactured goods	p^{M}	price of manufactured good
σ	Elasticity of substitution between manufactured varieties	p^{A}	price of agricultural good
α	Fixed labor input requirement of manufacturing firms	w	Wage of workers
β	Variable labor input requirement of manufacturing firms	G	Manufacturing price index
L	Total labor endowment	Y	Aggregate income
		q^{A}	Agricultural output
		q^{M}	Manufacturing output per firm
		n	Mass of manufacturing firms
		ω	Real wage

6. Advantages of general equilibrium modeling of monopolistic competition

Monopolistic competition accounts for some of the characteristics of modern industries, including product differentiation and a certain degree of market power among firms.

Although monopolistic competition is a form of imperfect competition, the firms, in the present model, are still atomistic in the sense that they do not take any strategic actions against each other. This simplifies the analysis and allows us to solve for equilibrium and determine industry characteristics such as individual firm size and firm mass within the industry.

The simplicity offers room for various kinds of applications in general equilibrium settings, as will be demonstrated in subsequent chapters. The next chapter features an entrepreneur specification of monopolistic competition that has implications for inequality and entry deterrence. Chapter 3 offers a theoretical account of the adoption of mass production in general equilibrium by introducing the technological choice of firms. Chapter 4 examines trade and competition policy in a setting in which two countries trade differentiated goods. Chapter 5 introduces the geographical mobility of people to explore the notion of natural advantage and the formation of a city. Finally, Chapter 6 describes the impact of globalization on cities by focusing on the location of corporate headquarters.

---

[i] The two are separable in the sense that the goods can be partitioned into groups so that preferences within groups can be described independently of the quantities in other groups, as explained by Deaton and Muellbauer (1980).

Chapter 2 Inequality and non-strategic entry deterrence in monopolistic competition

1. Introduction

Forslid and Ottaviano (2003) analyzed a model of monopolistic competition in which geographically mobile skilled workers are needed to set up firms. This model is now known as the footloose entrepreneur model and it explains the relation between inter-regional trade costs and agglomeration created by the migration of skilled workers. The model is included among the core models of the new economic geography literature.[ii]

This chapter demonstrates that the approach can also be used as a way to illustrate inequality in a general equilibrium setting. Three results are obtained. First, in the short-run with a given number of entrepreneurs, inequality between entrepreneurs and their employees exist in general and can infinitely increase. Inequality increases with low share of entrepreneurs and/or weak love of variety of consumers. Second, in the long-run when all agents are allowed to start businesses, equality will be achieved and the share of entrepreneurs in the economy will be determined only by preferences, i.e., love of variety: the stronger love of variety, the higher rate of participation in entrepreneurial activities. Third, comparison of short- and long-run results reveals that the entrepreneurs lose as the economy approaches the long-run equilibrium.

The short-run result suggests that there are both supply side and demand side reasons for inequality. The long-run result suggests that demand side characteristics may also explain differences observed in the extent of entrepreneurial activities between economies. The long-run equilibrium may not be realized, however. Conflict of interest may exist between existing and potential entrants, which may hinder entrepreneurial activities in the long run.

2. Short-run analysis

We abstract from the geographic aspects, i.e., regions and trade costs, of the Forslid and Ottaviano model and focus on the monopolistically competitive sector to analyze a single-sector general equilibrium model. The population of the economy is denoted as L. Members are either entrepreneurs or workers. The share of entrepreneurs within the population is denoted as e $(0 < e < 1)$, and is assumed to be fixed in the short-run. Correspondingly, the share of workers is $1-e$. The firms run by the entrepreneurs are assumed to be monopolistically competitive. Each entrepreneur employs workers to produce a particular variety. It is assumed that c units of workers are needed per unit output.

10   Chapter 2

The same population also comprises the consumers. The assumption for consumer behavior is a standard one, originally developed by Dixit and Stiglitz (1977). All consumers have the same preferences, which are defined as

$$U = \left[\int_0^n m(i)^\rho \, di \right]^{\frac{1}{\rho}},$$

where U is the composite of all the differentiated varieties, n is the mass of varieties, $m(i)$ is the consumption of variety i, and ρ is the substitution parameter. It is assumed that $0 < \rho < 1$ to ensure that the varieties are imperfect substitutes. $\sigma \equiv 1/(1-\rho) > 1$ represents the elasticity of substitution between any two varieties. Higher (lower) σ means weaker (stronger) love of variety. Denoting the price of a variety as $p(i)$, a price index

$$G \equiv \left[\int_0^n p(i)^{1-\sigma} \, di \right]^{\frac{1}{1-\sigma}} \tag{1}$$

is introduced such that total expenditure is GU. G is an overall level of prices that each firm takes as given.

In the above setting, consumers' utility maximization leads to demand for each variety being $p(i)^{-\sigma} G^{\sigma-1} Y$, where Y is aggregate income. Demand therefore depends not only on $p(i)$ and Y but also on G. Y consists of total profits earned by the entrepreneurs and total earnings of the workers. When π is profit of each firm and each worker's wage is set equal to 1,

$$Y = eL\pi + (1-e)L. \tag{2}$$

On the supply side, entrepreneurs of monopolistically competitive firms will set their prices so that marginal revenues equal marginal costs:

$$p(i)(1 - 1/\sigma) = c. \tag{3}$$

This is known as mark-up pricing in which firms always set their prices above their marginal costs, c. However, since rival firms are producing more or less substitutable varieties, the mark-up depends on σ: when the varieties are close substitutes (or consumers' love of variety is weak), i.e., when σ is high, then consumers are sensitive to prices and the prices become closer to c. By substituting Eq. (3) into (1), we find that the mark-up pricing by each firm leads to the price index being

$$G = n^{\frac{1}{1-\sigma}} \frac{\sigma c}{\sigma - 1}, \tag{4}$$

where

$$n = eL. \tag{5}$$

Further, denoting the output of each firm as $q(i)$, since the profit of each firm (π) is $p(i)q(i) - cq(i)$, using Eq. (3), we have

$$\pi = \frac{c}{\sigma - 1} q(i). \tag{6}$$

We can now consider the short-run equilibrium. It is defined as a situation in which the good and the factor markets clear (i.e. supply equals demand), at a given level of e. The good market clearing condition is

$$q(i) = p(i)^{-\sigma} G^{\sigma-1} Y, \tag{7}$$

and the factor market clearing condition is

$$L = n + ncq(i), \tag{8}$$

which means that the population (L) needs to match the amount of entrepreneurs and workers, i.e., those other than entrepreneurs must be fully employed as workers.

The short-run equilibrium can be obtained by solving Eqs. (7) and (8) simultaneously, after substituting Eqs. (2) through (6) into Eqs. (7) and (8). We then have

$$q(i) = \frac{1 - e}{ec} \tag{9}$$

which is the equilibrium output of each firm in the short-run. This means that the fewer entrepreneurs (and therefore fewer firms), the larger output (or size) of each firm. Substituting Eq. (9) into Eq. (6) gives the short-run equilibrium profit:

$$\pi = \frac{1 - e}{e(\sigma - 1)}. \tag{10}$$

Proposition 1. In the short-run, i.e., when the share of entrepreneurs (e) within the population is fixed, the profit of each firm (π) can take any positive value depending on e and the elasticity of substitution between any two varieties (σ): the lower e and/or the lower σ, the higher π.

Proposition 1 can intuitively be interpreted as follows. Imagine that only a smaller fraction of the population is allowed to be entrepreneurs. Then, other things being equal, each firm becomes larger (as shown in Eq. (9)) and correspondingly each firm's profit becomes larger (as shown in Eq. (6)). Continuing this leads to considering a tiny e close to 0: as $e \to 0$, $\pi \to \infty$. Also, imagine that the consumers' love of variety becomes stronger and the firms produce less similar or less substitutable varieties. Other things being equal, as shown in Eq. (3), this implies a higher mark-up and higher prices, leading to higher profits (as shown in Eq. (6)). Continuing this leads to considering a low σ very close to 1: as $\sigma \to 1$, $\pi \to \infty$.

12   Chapter 2

Here, in the short-run, each entrepreneur earns π, while each worker earns 1. Since both entrepreneurs and workers face the same prices, difference in their earnings imply difference in their utilities. (The indirect utilities for the entrepreneurs and the workers are π/G and $1/G$, respectively.) $\pi > 1$ ($\pi < 1$) means that the entrepreneurs' utilities are higher (lower) than those of the workers. Since there is no upper limit on π, in theory, inequality can increase infinitely.

3. Entry, exit, and long-run equilibrium

This section considers the long-run situation where e is no longer fixed, meaning that the population can choose occupations. Given the level of π, the workers now consider whether they also want to become entrepreneurs. Workers have incentives to do so if $\pi > 1$, that is, when existing entrepreneurs earn more than what the workers do. On the other hand, if $\pi < 1$, meaning that the entrepreneurs earn less than the workers, the entrepreneurs shut down their firms and become workers. In any case, entry or exit occur until $\pi = 1$. (Entry means the workers becoming entrepreneurs; exit means the entrepreneurs becoming workers.) Substituting $\pi = 1$ into Eq. (10) to solve for e, we have

$$e = 1/\sigma. \tag{11}$$

Proposition 2. In the long run, the share of entrepreneurs within the population (e) only depends on the elasticity of substitution between any two varieties (σ), and e is an inverse of σ.

$1/\sigma$ is the long-run or the maximum share of entrepreneurs in this model economy. σ, as defined in the outset, reflects the love of variety: stronger (weaker) love of variety implies lower (higher) σ. Proposition 2 can then be interpreted that when peoples' love of variety is strong (i.e. σ is low), more people in the population will become entrepreneurs, and therefore the economy will have more firms and varieties.

When the economy reaches the long-run equilibrium, both the entrepreneurs and the workers earn 1, and equality is achieved. It is important to note, however, that transition from the short- to the long-run equilibrium does not necessarily raise the utility of all. Suppose that initially $\pi > 1$ and entry occurs, i.e., the workers set up new firms and start their own businesses. How will this affect the welfare of the existing entrepreneurs? Since π decreases to 1 in the long-run, the existing entrepreneurs' utility changes from π/G_S in the short-run to $1/G_L$ in the long-run, where G_S is the price index in the short-run and G_L is the price index in the long-run. For the existing entrepreneurs to enjoy increased utility, therefore, it is necessary that $\pi/G_S < 1/G_L$. That is, using Eqs. (4), (10), and (11),

$$\pi\left(=\frac{1-e}{e(\sigma-1)}\right) < \frac{G_S}{G_L}\left(=(e\sigma)^{\frac{1}{1-\sigma}}\right). \tag{12}$$

Although the non-linearity keeps us from obtaining a full analysis, the following can be done, and it turns out that (12) does not hold. Differentiating the left and the right hand sides of (12) with respect to e, we obtain

$$\frac{\partial\pi}{\partial e} = -\frac{1}{e(\sigma-1)} - \frac{1-e}{e^2(\sigma-1)} \tag{13}$$

and

$$\frac{\partial(G_S/G_L)}{\partial e} = -\frac{\sigma(e\sigma)^{\frac{\sigma}{1-\sigma}}}{\sigma-1}. \tag{14}$$

Inspecting Eqs. (13) and (14), recalling that by assumption $0 < e < 1$ and $\sigma > 1$, we can confirm that $\partial\pi/\partial e < 0$ and $\partial(G_S/G_L)/\partial e < 0$. These imply that both π and G_S/G_L are decreasing in e. In addition, evaluating Eqs. (13) and (14) at $e = 1/\sigma$, we have

$$\frac{\partial\pi}{\partial e} = -\frac{\sigma^2}{\sigma-1} \quad \text{at } e = 1/\sigma \tag{15}$$

and

$$\frac{\partial(G_S/G_L)}{\partial e} = -\frac{\sigma}{\sigma-1} \quad \text{at } e = 1/\sigma. \tag{16}$$

Comparing Eqs. (15) and (16), since $\sigma > 1$,

$$\left|\frac{-\sigma^2}{\sigma-1}\right| > \left|\frac{-\sigma}{\sigma-1}\right|$$

which implies that the slope of π is steeper than that of G_S/G_L at $e = 1/\sigma$. We have, therefore, $\pi > G_S/G_L$, i.e., $\pi/G_S > 1/G_L$, at least in the neighborhood of the long-run equilibrium (i.e. $e = 1/\sigma$). These results are jointly illustrated in Figure 2.1.

Proposition 3. If $\pi > 1$ then as the economy approaches the long-run equilibrium (i.e. $\pi = 1$ and $e = 1/\sigma$), the existing entrepreneurs' utility decreases.

Proposition 3 can be interpreted as follows. On the one hand, entry improves the utility of all because the new firms provide new varieties, reflected as a fall in the price index, G. On the other hand, however, entry also means tougher competition for the existing entrepreneurs, so each firm's output falls and correspondingly profit falls. As the

14   Chapter 2

economy approaches the long-run equilibrium in which there are already increased number of entrepreneurs and rival firms, the latter effect outweighs the former; gains from variety increase cannot compensate for the loss in the existing entrepreneurs' profits.

The result that the existing entrepreneurs lose from new entry suggests that existing entrepreneurs could work to block new entry. In the present monopolistic competition setting, they all have incentives to deter entry in non-strategic ways, for example, through voting for entry-restricting policies. If that happens, the economy could get trapped in low entrepreneurial participations (i.e. $e < 1/\sigma$) and high inequality (i.e. $\pi > 1$), before reaching the long-run equilibrium.

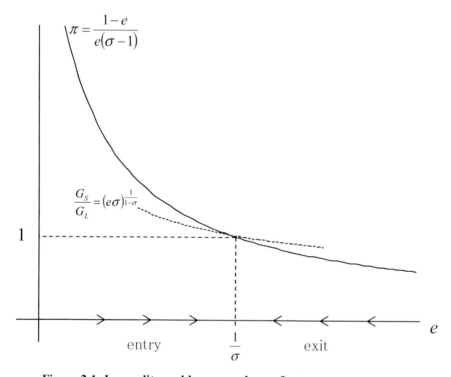

Figure 2.1: Inequality and long-run share of entrepreneurs

4. Concluding remarks for Chapter 2

There is growing interest throughout the world regarding inequality. This chapter presented one way of illustrating inequality using a monopolistic competition model with entrepreneurs. The short-run result in Proposition 1 indicates that there are both supply side and demand side reasons for inequality. Restriction to entry into business, for example, implies a lower e and increases inequality. At the same time, weaker love of variety, i.e., smaller σ, will also increase inequality.

Surveys on entrepreneurial activities indicate some variation in the ratios of the population taking part in entrepreneurial activities between economies. According to the estimates by the Global Entrepreneurship Monitor (2014), for example, those taking part in early-stage or established entrepreneurial activities within the adult population are 10.5% and 11.0% in Germany and Japan, respectively, versus higher rates in the United Kingdom (17.3%) and the United States (20.7%).

There are various reasons that may explain the variation. Supply side explanations include heterogeneous agents, policy or business practices that restrict entry, and differences in entrepreneurial spirit between societies. While there are numerous possible supply side reasons explaining the variation, what can be learned from the long-run result in Proposition 2 is that *only* the demand side characteristics, that is, in the present model, the love of variety, determine the upper-bound share of entrepreneurs, when inequality is eliminated. Therefore, economies could have different levels of entrepreneurial activities even in their long-run equilibria.

Estimates of σ allow us to calculate long-run shares of entrepreneurs using Proposition 2. How does the prediction from the model compare to real world data? Broda and Weinstein (2006) provide us with estimates of σ for some industries in the United States. While values of σ differ by industry, the median value of σ from their study is 2.55 and their simple average is 4.65 for the period 1990 to 2001. The predicted upper-bound shares of entrepreneurs from the present model using these values are 39.2% and 21.5%, respectively. These are not too off the mark compared to the above-mentioned share of 20.7% for the United States.

Proposition 3 suggests that conflict of interest exists between the existing and new entrepreneurs. Existing entrepreneurs are unlikely to accept new entry given that their economic welfare can be expected to deteriorate. Such opposition suggests that the long-run equilibrium may not be achieved, and economies may be trapped in situations where low participation rates in entrepreneurial activities and high inequalities coexist. A full analysis of this, however, would require a larger model with a political process.

[ii] See Baldwin et al. (2003) on the core models developed in the new economic geography literature.

Chapter 3 Making sense of the diffusion of mass production: a theoretical account of the rise of mass production

1. Introduction

Mass production has been intensively studied in the business world. The term mass production is used frequently, but it is usually associated with Ford Motor Company's automobile production in the early twentieth century, sometimes called Fordism. Introducing revolutionary ways of production must have affected people's economic life in many ways, both in their workplaces and in their consumption. The way people work changed drastically and consumer goods became standardized and cheaper.

While these production methods faced various kinds of opposition, including that from popular figures such as Charlie Chaplin in his critical film "Modern Times," mass production eventually diffused throughout the industrialized world during the twentieth century. Other automobile manufacturers adopted Ford's assembly line production style. The techniques have also been applied to many other products, including "white goods" such as refrigerators and washing machines. Mass production became, in the words of Sabel and Zeitlin (1985, p133), "the undisputed emblem of industrial efficiency." It should be noted, however, that mass production did not work in all industries. According to Hounshell (1984) early application of mass production to housing, furniture, and agricultural goods production turned out to be unsuccessful.

The mass production system is characterized by its assembly line, which was made possible by the introduction of interchangeable parts made by steel punches and presses. Its rise seems inevitable today, but it was revolutionary in the early twentieth century when Ford started mass producing Model Ts. Ford's famous Model T automobile displayed drastic price drops and rapid production increases. When the car was introduced in the market in 1908, its retail price was 850 dollars. Ford sold 5,986 units. After introducing its revolutionary assembly line in 1913, the Model T cost 360 dollars, and 577,036 units were sold in 1916.[iii]

Prior to mass production, when there were no assembly lines, manufacturing relied on the "fitting" done by many skilled workers. Some departures from this pattern were seen in the United States in its small arms production, sewing machine production by Singer, agricultural machinery (such as reapers and mowers) by McCormick, and bicycle production.[iv] But it was Ford that combined the two elements of mass production, interchangeable parts and minute division of labor, to make moving assembly line production a reality.

Running the assembly line also required organizational changes. Freeman and Soete

18   Chapter 3

(1997, p.144) describe "[T]he need for skilled workers was reduced to a minimum and the plant was controlled and co-ordinated by the new profession of industrial (production) engineers and an army of foremen and indirect workers responding to their orders." This suggests that as firms introduced assembly lines they needed to hire more people to manage the system, which is likely to have increased their fixed costs.

In business studies, interest shifted long ago from mass production to new concepts such as lean production, flexible/agile production, and mass customization, etc.[v] This shift, to some extent, was triggered by the rise of Japanese manufacturing in the post-war era. Japan's production system has gone beyond mass production.[vi] Womack et al. (1990) studied it to come up with the concept of lean production. Pine (1993) addressed the management issues of how to mass-produce and individually customize goods and services.

Within the literature, however, mass production has not been addressed and rigorously studied from the viewpoint of economic theory. This study is an attempt to fill that gap. It aims to construct a formal model of mass production and then analyzes the transition from traditional, small-scale production to mass production. The model must be capable of capturing changes in firms' production scales as well as the welfare implications of the resulting standardization of consumer goods. To this aim use of monopolistic competition is proposed, because it is useful in capturing such supply and demand side changes. Specifically, the simplest possible general equilibrium model of monopolistic competition with technological choice is used. All firms initially produce using traditional technology. They are then given a new technology, mass production, and choose the more profitable one. It is shown that, consistent with intuition, transition to mass production occurs if the expected gains in operating profits exceed the required increase in fixed costs for the new production system. Once the transition to mass production takes place, there is no reversal to traditional, small-scale production unless preferences change. It is also shown that such a transition of the economy to mass production, driven by profit-seeking firms' decisions to adopt new mass production technologies, always improves welfare. These findings may increase our understanding of some of the underlying forces that drove the diffusion of mass production in the twentieth century.

The rest of the chapter is organized as follows. After setting the technological assumptions in Section 2, the initial equilibrium is derived in Section 3. Section 4 explains the conditions under which firms adopt mass production technology, and a new mass production equilibrium is derived and analyzed. Welfare implications of the transition to mass production are presented in Section 5. The effects of the change in preferences after the transition to mass production is analyzed in Section 6, followed by a conclusion section that contains a brief summary and limitations of the analysis.

2. Technology choices

In the business literature, mass production is seen as a production system using assembly lines coupled with organizational changes that require more indirect workers to manage production. To formalize mass production, it is interpreted as a new production technology that requires larger fixed costs but reduces the marginal costs of production, compared to existing or traditional technology. Mass production would also require a variety of resources that differ from traditional production technology. For simplicity, however, this model assumes labor as the only factor of production. (Therefore, labor should not be interpreted literally, but should be interpreted as a composite of various production factors including labor.) Assuming fixed costs implies that the production technology exhibits increasing returns to scale. Specifically, as shown in Table 3.1, it is assumed that traditional technology requires F units of labor and c units of labor per unit output. Then denoting a firm's output as q, its cost function under traditional technology is $C(q) = F + cq$. On the other hand, mass production technology requires αF units of labor and βc units of labor per unit output, where importantly $\alpha > 1$ and $0 < \beta < 1$. This implies that switching to mass production reduces the marginal cost from c to βc, but requires an increase in fixed cost from F to αF. The cost function under mass production technology is $C(q) = \alpha F + \beta cq$.

Table 3.1: Technology choices

	fixed cost	marginal cost
traditional production	F	c
mass production	$\alpha F \ (\alpha > 1)$	$\beta c \ (0 < \beta < 1)$

3. Initial equilibrium with traditional technology

The population of the economy, or the total amount of production factors, is denoted as L. All members of the economy work and consume. Firms are assumed to be monopolistically competitive. Each firm produces a particular variety of goods. The mass of the firms is large enough so that there are no strategic interactions between the firms. There is some degree of competition, however, because other rival firms produce similar goods. We use a standard assumption for consumer behavior originally developed by Dixit and Stiglitz (1977). All consumers have the same preferences, which are defined as

$$U = \left[\int_0^n m(i)^\rho \, di \right]^{1/\rho},$$

where U is the composite of all the differentiated varieties, n is the mass of varieties, $m(i)$ is the consumption of variety i, and ρ is the substitution parameter. It is assumed that $0 < \rho < 1$ to ensure that the varieties are imperfect substitutes. $\sigma \equiv 1/(1-\rho) > 1$ represents the elasticity of substitution between any two varieties. σ increases as desire for variety decreases. Denoting the price of a variety as $p(i)$, a price index

$$G \equiv \left[\int_0^n p(i)^{1-\sigma} di \right]^{\frac{1}{1-\sigma}} \tag{1}$$

is introduced such that total expenditure is GU. G is the overall level of prices that each firm takes as given.

In the above setting, consumers' utility maximization leads to demand for each variety being $p(i)^{-\sigma} G^{\sigma-1} Y$, where Y is aggregate income. Demand therefore depends not only on $p(i)$ and Y but also on G.

On the supply side, a typical monopolistically competitive firm will set its price so that marginal revenue equals marginal cost (c), that is,

$$p_T (1 - 1/\sigma) = c, \tag{2}$$

which is known as mark-up pricing, where firms always set their prices above their marginal costs. (Hereafter, i will be omitted, and subscripts T and M will be used to denote traditional technology and mass production technology, respectively.) Since rival firms are producing more or less substitutable varieties, the mark-up depends on σ: when the varieties are close substitutes (or the consumers' love of variety is weak), i.e., when σ is high, then the consumers are sensitive to price and they come closer to c. By substituting Eq. (2) into Eq. (1), we find that mark-up pricing by each firm leads to the price index being

$$G_T = (n_T)^{\frac{1}{1-\sigma}} \frac{\sigma c}{\sigma - 1}. \tag{3}$$

We can now consider the equilibrium with traditional technology. It is defined as a situation in which, allowing free entry, the goods and factor markets clear (i.e., supply equals demand). The profit of a typical firm (π_T) is

$$\pi_T = p_T q_T - F - c q_T. \tag{4}$$

Free entry, however, drives π_T down to zero. Substituting Eq. (2) into Eq. (4) and setting it equal to zero, we have

$$q_T = \frac{F(\sigma-1)}{c}. \tag{5}$$

The goods market clearing condition is

$$q_T = p_T^{-\sigma} G_T^{\sigma-1} Y, \tag{6}$$

where Y is equal to the total earnings of the workers. Setting the wage (or the returns on the factors of production) equal to 1, then $Y = L$. The factor market clearing condition is

$$L = n_T F + n_T c q_T, \tag{7}$$

which means that the population (L) needs to be fully employed. Substituting Eq. (5) into Eq. (7) and solving, we have

$$n_T = \frac{L}{F\sigma}. \tag{8}$$

Substituting Eq. (8) into Eq. (6) can be confirmed to lead to the same result as Eq. (5).

4. Transition to mass production

The equilibrium derived above is the standard result of monopolistic competition in general equilibrium. We move on to consider the behavior of firms when they can choose mass production technology as given in Table 3.1. Given mass production technology, a typical firm calculates its hypothetical profit ($\tilde{\pi}_M$), which is its expected profit if it adopts mass production technology. Denoting the hypothetical price and output as $\tilde{p}_M$ and $\tilde{q}_M$, respectively,

$$\tilde{\pi}_M = \tilde{p}_M \tilde{q}_M - \alpha F - \beta c \tilde{q}_M, \tag{9}$$

where

$$\tilde{p}_M = \frac{\sigma \beta c}{\sigma-1} \tag{10}$$

and

$$\tilde{q}_M = \tilde{p}_M^{-\sigma} G_T^{\sigma-1} Y. \tag{11}$$

Note in Eq. (11) that the price index is G_T. This is because firms can only set the prices of their own varieties and take the price index, which is the overall price level including rival firms' prices, as given. Because the firms are symmetric and because there are no strategic interactions among them, hereafter, we focus on the typical firm. Substituting Eqs. (10) and (11) into Eq. (9) and rearranging we have

$$\tilde{\pi}_M = F\left(\beta^{1-\sigma} - \alpha\right). \tag{12}$$

Profit-seeking firms compare π_T (which is zero) and $\tilde{\pi}_M$, and switch to mass production if $\tilde{\pi}_M > \pi_T \left(=0\right)$. That is, firms' profitable deviation from the traditional to mass production occur if $F\left(\beta^{1-\sigma} - \alpha\right) > 0$ or

$$\alpha < \beta^{1-\sigma}. \tag{13}$$

22   Chapter 3

Result 1. Given the mass production technology parameters α and β, the transition to mass production takes place when $\alpha < \beta^{1-\sigma}$.

Interpreting condition (13) requires inspection of the hypothetical profit ($\tilde{\pi}_M$) shown in Eq. (9). $\tilde{\pi}_M$ can be rearranged as $\tilde{\pi}_M = \left(\tilde{p}_M - \beta c\right)\tilde{q}_M - \alpha F$, where $\left(\tilde{p}_M - \beta c\right)\tilde{q}_M$ is the expected operating profit (i.e., sales minus variable cost), and αF is the fixed cost if the firm switched to mass production. The expected operating profit is the product of the expected operating profit per unit ($\tilde{p}_M - \beta c$) and hypothetical demand ($\tilde{q}_M$). On the one hand, because the new technology is defined to reduce the marginal cost (c) by a factor of β, the profit-maximizing price will also be reduced by a factor of β as shown in Eq. (10). Hence, by switching to mass production the operating profit per unit is expected to be reduced by a factor of β. On the other hand, however, the price reduction is expected to increase demand by a factor of $\beta^{-\sigma}$, which can be confirmed by comparing q_T in Eq. (6) and $\tilde{q}_M$ in Eq. (11).[vii] Therefore, the net effect is that the operating profit is expected to increase by a factor of $\beta \cdot \beta^{-\sigma}$, i.e., $\beta^{1-\sigma} \left(>1\right)$. Then condition (13) can be interpreted as meaning that in order for the transition to mass production to take place, the new technology must be such that the firms' expected rate of increase in operating profits ($\beta^{1-\sigma}$) exceeds the rate of increase in fixed costs (α).

Result 1 means, consistent with intuition, that the lower α and/or the lower β is, the more likely the economy will be to switch to mass production. Also, other things being equal, a higher σ means a greater likelihood of the transition to mass production. That is, economies with firms producing relatively homogeneous goods are more likely to switch to mass production. With the present model, therefore, the reasons why mass production was more successfully applied in some industries (like in "white goods" such as refrigerators and washing machines) than in others (like in housing, furniture, and agricultural goods) are both technological and demand-side related. Mass production did not work in housing, furniture, and agricultural goods because the technology was not profitable enough for firms and/or consumers had a stronger love of variety (i.e., lower σ) in these goods than in refrigerators and washing machines.

Condition (13) is illustrated in Figure 3.1. Differentiating $\beta^{1-\sigma}$ with respect to β gives $(1-\sigma)\beta^{-\sigma} < 0$, so $\beta^{1-\sigma}$ is decreasing in β. Thus, plotting $\beta^{1-\sigma}$ against β gives a downward-sloping curve. At a given level of α, the range of β that satisfies condition (13) and leads to the transition to mass production is shown by the thick solid line. Lowering the level of α will expand the range of β that satisfies condition (13), which makes the transition to mass production more likely. Note that a higher σ

essentially rotates the $\beta^{1-\sigma}$ curve clockwise as shown by the dotted lines, which will extend the thick solid line, also making the transition to mass production more likely.

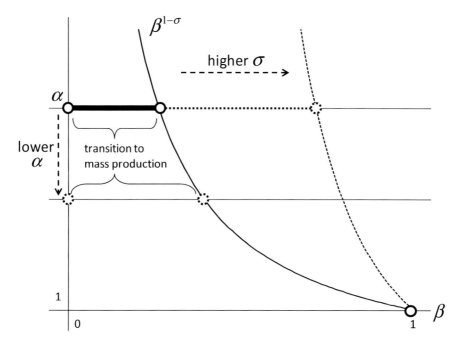

Figure 3.1: Transition to mass production

The new equilibrium with mass production is obtained as follows, similar to the way the initial equilibrium was found. A typical profit-maximizing firm sets the price of the variety it produces as

$$p_M = \frac{\sigma \beta c}{\sigma - 1}. \tag{14}$$

So the price index is

$$G_M = (n_M)^{\frac{1}{1-\sigma}} \frac{\sigma \beta c}{\sigma - 1}. \tag{15}$$

The profit of a typical firm (π_M) is

$$\pi_M = p_M q_M - \alpha F - \beta c q_M, \tag{16}$$

but free entry drives π_M down to zero. Hence, substituting Eq. (14) into Eq. (16) and setting it equal to zero, we have

$$q_M = \frac{\alpha F (\sigma - 1)}{\beta c}. \tag{17}$$

24　Chapter 3

The goods market clearing condition is

$$q_M = p_M{}^{-\sigma} G_M{}^{\sigma-1} Y, \qquad (18)$$

and the factor market clearing condition is

$$L = n_M \alpha F + n_M \beta c q_M. \qquad (19)$$

Substituting Eq. (17) into Eq. (19) and solving, we have

$$n_M = \frac{L}{\alpha F \sigma}, \qquad (20)$$

and we can confirm that substituting Eq. (20) into Eq. (18) leads to the same result as Eq. (17).

The endogenous variables in the two equilibria derived so far are summarized in Table 3.2. Comparing the two, it is found that the prices are lower ($p_T > p_M$), and each firm is larger ($q_T < q_M$) but there are fewer firms ($n_T > n_M$) in the mass production equilibrium. So it can be said that the result captures some of the features of mass production: products are "standardized" in the sense that fewer varieties are produced in larger quantities by bigger firms. Since the prices are lowered (which lowers G) but the number of firms and varieties drop (which raises G), the net effect on the price index (G) is ambiguous. (This will be addressed in the welfare analysis in Section 5.)

Table 3.2: Comparison of the two equilibria

	traditional production (initial)	mass production
p	$p_T = \dfrac{\sigma c}{\sigma - 1}$	$p_M = \dfrac{\sigma \beta c}{\sigma - 1}$
G	$G_T = \left(\dfrac{L}{\sigma F}\right)^{\frac{1}{1-\sigma}} \dfrac{\sigma c}{\sigma - 1}$	$G_M = \left(\dfrac{L}{\sigma \alpha F}\right)^{\frac{1}{1-\sigma}} \dfrac{\sigma \beta c}{\sigma - 1}$
q	$q_T = \dfrac{F(\sigma - 1)}{c}$	$q_M = \dfrac{\alpha F(\sigma - 1)}{\beta c}$
n	$n_T = \dfrac{L}{F\sigma}$	$n_M = \dfrac{L}{\alpha F \sigma}$

Is the mass production equilibrium stable? Assume that condition (13) is satisfied, i.e., $\alpha < \beta^{1-\sigma}$, and the transition to mass production took place. But the firms are still free to choose the traditional technology. If a typical firm switches back to the traditional technology (when all the rest of the firms are producing with mass production technology), its hypothetical profit ($\tilde{\pi}_T$) is

$$\tilde{\pi}_T = \left(\tilde{p}_T - c\right)\tilde{q}_T - F .$$

(21)

where

$$\tilde{p}_T = \frac{\sigma c}{\sigma - 1}$$

(22)

and

$$\tilde{q}_T = \tilde{p}_T^{-\sigma} G_M^{\sigma-1} Y .$$

(23)

Inspecting Eqs. (21) to (23), it is seen that $\tilde{\pi}_T$ cannot be positive: Adopting traditional technology implies that the marginal cost (c) and, correspondingly, the profit maximizing price will increase by a factor of $1/\beta$ (obtained by comparing $\tilde{p}_T$ in Eq. (22) and p_M in Eq. (14)). Hence, the operating profit per unit is expected to increase by a factor of $1/\beta$, compared to the operating profit per unit under mass production technology. However, because of the price increase, demand is expected to decrease by a factor of $1/\beta^{-\sigma}$ (obtained by comparing $\tilde{q}_T$ in Eq. (23) and q_M in Eq. (18)). The net effect is that operating profit is expected to decrease by a factor of $\left(1/\beta\right) \cdot \left(1/\beta^{-\sigma}\right)$, i.e., $1/\beta^{1-\sigma}$. Fixed cost drops by a factor of $1/\alpha$ when a firm re-adopts the traditional technology. Then a firm can profitably depart from mass production and re-adopt the traditional technology if the rate of loss of operating profits ($1/\beta^{1-\sigma}$) is more than compensated for by the rate of reduction in fixed costs ($1/\alpha$). That is, $1/\beta^{1-\sigma} > 1/\alpha$, i.e., $\alpha > \beta^{1-\sigma}$. This is not possible, because we assumed $\alpha < \beta^{1-\sigma}$.

Result 2. The mass production equilibrium is stable.

Result 2 implies that once the transition from traditional technology to mass production has taken place, it is not in the interest of firms to go back; there is no reversal to the traditional equilibrium.

5. Mass production for consumers

Suppose that condition (13) is satisfied, and that firms adopt the mass production technology, driving the economy's transition to mass production. Is this good for consumers? The transition to mass production always reduces prices, which itself is welfare improving. At the same time, however, since mass production technology requires larger fixed costs, meaning that more resources are now needed to set up a firm, there will be fewer firms in the economy, which implies there will be less variety for consumers. (Thus, some degree of "standardization" is inevitable.) From the consumers' point of view, therefore, there is a tradeoff between lower prices and less variety. We need, then, to compare welfare under traditional production and mass production equilibria.

26   Chapter 3

In the initial equilibrium with the traditional technology, indirect utility was $1/G_T$. After the transition to mass production it became $1/G_M$. These two expressions are the measures of welfare in this model. Consumers enjoy increased welfare as long as $1/G_M > 1/G_T$, i.e., $G_M < G_T$. Using the expressions for G_T and G_M given in Table 3.2, consumers' condition for welfare improvement is found to be

$$\alpha < \beta^{1-\sigma}, \tag{24}$$

which is exactly the same as condition (13). This implies that the transition to mass production, when it takes place, is always welfare improving.

Result 3. The condition for the transition to mass production (Result 1) is equivalent to the condition for consumers' welfare improvement.

Condition (24) appears to be the same as condition (13), but has a different meaning. Inspecting the price indices G_T and G_M reveals that a transition to mass production implies that, on one hand, the numbers of firms and varieties are reduced by a factor of $1/\alpha$, which increases the price index by a factor of $(1/\alpha)^{1/(1-\sigma)}$.

On the other hand, the prices of individual varieties are reduced by a factor of β, which reduces the price index by a factor of β. Then, for consumers to gain, welfare gained from the drop in prices must outweigh the negative effect of the loss of variety so that $(1/\alpha)^{1/(1-\sigma)} \beta < 1$, that is, $\alpha < \beta^{1-\sigma}$. Condition (24), therefore, means that for consumers to gain from the transition to mass production, losses from decreased overall variety must be more than compensated for by gains from reductions in the prices of the individual varieties.

6. Changes in preferences and mass production

The results so far have been obtained focusing on technological change and choice. It is also possible, however, for consumers' preferences to change. Specifically, the effect of a change in the elasticity of substitution (σ) on the choice of technology can be analyzed. This is relevant to the successful challenge by General Motors (GM) against Ford in the 1920s. When the market became flooded with low price/standardized Model T Fords, GM succeeded by introducing a wide range of different types of cars that attracted customers. It may be that consumers at the time got bored with the much cheaper but standardized cars that Ford produced, and GM took advantage of that by increasing the varieties of cars.[viii] The so-called quartz shock in the wristwatch industry in the 1970s offers another example. Japanese watchmakers came up with a way to mass-produce quartz watches which were much cheaper and more accurate than traditional mechanical watches. The shock hit the traditional mechanical watchmakers hard, including those in Switzerland, but later a revival of traditional mechanical watch production was seen. Again, it may be said that consumers got bored with the cheap but standardized watches. In the present model, some of this can be captured by assuming that consumers' preferences changed, with their desire for variety getting stronger, i.e., as a decrease in σ.

Suppose that the transition to mass production has taken place, so that condition (13), i.e., $\alpha < \beta^{1-\sigma}$, is satisfied. Consider then that the consumers' desire for variety becomes stronger (because they become bored with the cheap standardized goods). σ thus decreases from σ to $\sigma*$ ($\sigma > \sigma*$). As already derived in Result 2, firms can profitably return to traditional production if $\alpha > \beta^{1-\sigma*}$. Therefore, a return to traditional production occurs if both $\alpha < \beta^{1-\sigma}$ and $\alpha > \beta^{1-\sigma*}$ are satisfied. That is,

$$\beta^{1-\sigma*} < \alpha < \beta^{1-\sigma}. \tag{25}$$

Result 4. Return to traditional production can occur when consumers' love of variety increases.

Condition (25) is diagrammatically shown in Figure 3.2. The return from mass production to traditional production occurs if σ decreases from σ to $\sigma*$ and β is within the range illustrated by the thick solid line. If β is lower than that range, returning to traditional production is not profitable for firms, and they choose to carry on with mass production. This is because the expected loss in operating profits is too large to be compensated for by the reduction in fixed costs obtained by returning to traditional production.

28   Chapter 3

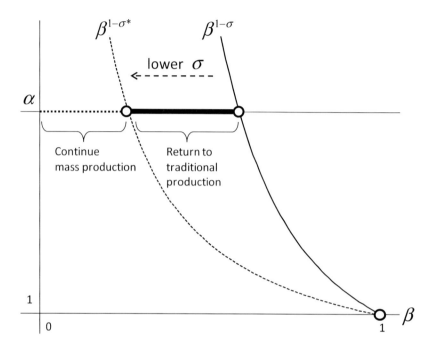

Figure 3.2: Return to traditional production

7. Summary and remarks for Chapter 3

This chapter used monopolistic competition to study mass production from an economic theory perspective. The first result was quite intuitive. The transition to mass production occurs if the expected gains in operating profits exceed the necessary increase in fixed costs. Also, other things being equal, mass production is more likely to be adopted when firms are producing relatively homogeneous goods (Result 1). Second, it was also found that once such a transition to mass production has taken place there will be no going back to traditional technology (Result 2). The third result was that the adoption of mass production driven by profit-seeking firms is always welfare improving (Result 3). Finally, the analysis showed that an increase in the consumers' love of variety can lead to a return from mass production to traditional production (Result 4).

    The second result implies that once a profitable, large-scale method of production is invented, all firms will adopt it and the old technology will be left behind; it is in no firm's interest to go back to the old technology. This suggests that workers had to go through various changes and experience costly adjustments. But the third result, that mass production is always welfare improving, suggests that there was something that may have more or less compensated for their hardship. It may also suggest that viewing mass production in only a negative manner, as if the resulting "standardization" deprives people of choice/variety is one-sided and not correct. A combination of the second and third results may help our understanding of why mass production diffused worldwide during the twentieth century despite workers' opposition. Mass production may well have had various negative impacts on workplaces, but there were also compensating positive impacts on consumers that could have outweighed the negative impacts.

There are a number of limitations to the present model due to its simplicity. First, technology is given, so the model does not explain what brings the mass production technology. Second, by using a single-factor model, potential disutilities or adjustment costs for workers who had to move to different workplaces and/or change the work that they performed were omitted. Third, the model is that of a single industry, and richer results may well be obtained from a multi-industry model. Fourth, new investment required for mass production is only modeled as an increase in fixed costs, so the sectors that supplied the assembly lines and machines needed to produce interchangeable parts are not explicitly modeled.

[iii] These figures are complied and provided by Hounshell (1984, Table 6.1.).

[iv] See, for example, Bo (1984) on the development of machine tools that preceded the rise of mass production. See also Hounsell (1984) on the rise and transition to mass production in the United States.

[v] See, for example, Duguay et al. (1997) on flexible/agile production.

[vi] See, for example, Kenney and Florida (1988) on mass production in Japan and the society.

[vii] Here, a higher σ corresponds to a larger expected demand increase because higher σ implies that the consumers' love of variety is weaker and that they are more sensitive to prices.

[viii] To be exact, GM did not actually return to traditional production as in the model, but introduced a new corporate structure in which the company is divided into divisions. Each division specialized in a particular segment of the market, as if the divisions were different companies, and supplied models that were suitable to each segment. See Freeman and Soete (1997, 6.3) on this.

Competition policy   31

Chapter 4 Competition policy in a globalized world: how does a policy taken by one country work in a globalized world?

1. Introduction

How do competition policies of individual economies work in a globalized world? This chapter analyzes the consequence of entry regulation introduced by one country in a world where goods are freely traded.

The model used for the analysis is that of two symmetric countries with two industries, the M industry and the A industry. The firms in the M industry, which are producing differentiated goods, are monopolistically competitive and those in the A industry are perfectly competitive. Free international trade is assumed in both industries. Under this set up, the analysis proceeds assuming that one country, the foreign country, introduces a policy regulating entry in the M industry.

Free trade in the A industry equalizes the wages in the two countries, and consumers in both countries equally gain from having access to both varieties of the M good produced locally and imported. What happens when one country takes on a policy of regulating the mass of firms in the M industry? Previewing the results, it is shown that such a policy will not affect world welfare. Entry regulation reduces the mass of firms and varieties of goods supplied locally in the regulating country, but the existence of international trade induces the same mass of firm entry in the other country. The only change seen is the corresponding asymmetry of industrial structures in the two countries. The analysis may help to increase our understanding of the consequences of economic policies in today's globalized world.

The rest of the chapter is organized as follows. After presenting the assumptions of the analysis in Section 2, consumer and firm behaviors are derived in Section 3. In Section 4, three different equilibria are derived and compared. The first is the autarkic equilibrium, that is, equilibrium without international trade. The second is the trading equilibrium without entry regulation. The third equilibrium studied is the one in which the foreign country introduces a policy of entry regulation. Section 5 is the conclusion.

2. Assumptions

There are two countries which are of equal size and have the same economic structure. Each country has a population of L. There are two industries, the M industry and the A industry. The M industry produces differentiated goods, and the A industry produces homogenous goods. Firms in the M industry are assumed to be monopolistically competitive. Firms in the A industry are assumed to be perfectly

32   Chapter 4

competitive. Labor is the only factor of production in the model. Setting up a firm in the M industry requires F units of labor and c units of labor per output. There are no fixed costs required in the A industry, but a unit of labor is needed per unit output. Labor is not mobile internationally but is mobile between industries M and A.

All members of the economy work and consume. They are assumed to have the same preferences described by the following two tier structure:

$$U = M^\mu A^{1-\mu} \quad (0 < \mu < 1) \tag{1}$$

$$M = \left[\int_0^n m(i)^\rho \, di \right]^{\frac{1}{\rho}} \quad (0 < \rho < 1) \tag{2}$$

The upper tier (1) is a Cobb-Douglas function of the consumption of an aggregate of the varieties of the M good and the consumption of the A good. The second tier (2) defines M to be a CES (constant elasticity of substitution) function where $m(i)$ is the consumption of each variety i of the M good. M is therefore a CES composite of the total mass of varieties n. Since each firm in the M industry produces its own variety, n is also equal to the mass of firms in the M industry. The elasticity of substitution between any variety of the M good is $1/(1-\rho) \equiv \sigma \quad (\sigma > 1)$.

3. Consumer and firm behavior

Consumer behavior

Given income Y, the price of the A good p^A, and the price of each variety of the M good $p(i)$, the consumer's problem is to maximize her utility subject to the budget constraint

$$\int_0^n p(i)m(i)di + p^A A = Y. \tag{3}$$

As derived in Chapter 1, the demand functions for variety j of the M good and the A good are

$$m(j) = p(j)^{-\sigma} G^{\sigma-1} \mu Y, \tag{4}$$

and

$$A = \frac{(1-\mu)Y}{p^A}, \tag{5}$$

respectively, where the price index G is

$$G \equiv \left[\int_0^n p(i)^{\frac{\rho}{\rho-1}} \, di \right]^{\frac{\rho-1}{\rho}} = \left[\int_0^n p(i)^{1-\sigma} \, di \right]^{\frac{1}{1-\sigma}}. \tag{6}$$

Firm behavior

Each firm in the M industry produces a particular variety of the M good, but there is some degree of competition because other rival firms produce similar goods. A typical monopolistically competitive firm will set its price so that marginal revenue equals marginal cost, that is,

$$p(1-1/\sigma) = cw, \qquad (7)$$

where w is the wage. This is known as mark-up pricing, where firms always set their prices above their marginal costs. (Hereafter, i will be omitted.) Since rival firms are producing more or less substitutable varieties, the mark-up depends on σ: when the varieties are close substitutes (or the consumers' love of variety is weak), i.e., when σ is high, then the consumers are sensitive to price and they come closer to c. By substituting (7) into (6), we find that mark-up pricing by each firm leads to the price index being

$$G = n^{\frac{1}{1-\sigma}} \frac{\sigma cw}{\sigma-1}. \qquad (8)$$

4. Equilibrium

Autarkic equilibrium

We can now consider the equilibrium. We first consider equilibrium without international trade. It is defined as a situation in which, allowing free entry, the goods and factor markets clear (i.e., supply equals demand). The profit of a typical firm (π) is

$$\pi = pq - (F + cq)w. \qquad (9)$$

Free entry, however, drives π down to zero. Substituting (7) into (9) and setting it equal to zero, we have

$$q = \frac{F(\sigma-1)}{c}, \qquad (10)$$

which is the equilibrium firm output. The market clearing condition of the M good is

$$q = \mu p^{-\sigma} G^{\sigma-1} Y, \qquad (11)$$

where Y is equal to the total earnings of the workers. In the A industry perfect competition leads to the price of the A good (p^A) being equal to its marginal cost of production which is the wage. Then setting $p^A = 1$, we have $w = 1$. Hence, $Y = L$. Using (5), total demand for the A good is simply $(1-\mu)L$. The factor market clearing condition is therefore

$$L = nF + ncq + (1-\mu)L, \qquad (12)$$

which means that the population (L) needs to be fully employed. Substituting (10) into (12) and solving, we have

34   Chapter 4

$$n = \frac{\mu L}{F\sigma}.$$ (13)

It can be confirmed that substituting (13) into (11) leads to the same result as (10). Substituting (13) into (8), the price index in the autarkic equilibrium is found to be

$$G = \left(\frac{\mu L}{F\sigma}\right)^{\frac{1}{1-\sigma}} \frac{\sigma c}{\sigma - 1}.$$ (14)

Trading equilibrium

Next, we consider the equilibrium in which the two countries freely trade both the M and the A goods. The zero profit condition leaves (10) unaffected. The market clearing condition of the M good is also the same as in (11), but with two economies the price index becomes

$$G = \left(n_H + n_F\right)^{\frac{1}{1-\sigma}} \frac{\sigma c}{\sigma - 1}.$$ (15)

(Hereafter, subscripts H and F are used to stand for home and foreign, respectively.) The A good, the homogenous good, is freely traded internationally, so the wages equal to one in both countries. Therefore, the national income in each country is equal to L, that is, $Y_H = Y_F = L$. Then global income (Y) is

$$Y = Y_H + Y_F = 2L.$$ (16)

The factor market clearing condition is

$$2L = n_H F + n_H cq + n_F F + n_F cq + (1-\mu)Y.$$ (17)

Substituting (10) and (16) into (17) and solving, we have

$$n_H + n_F = \frac{2\mu L}{F\sigma},$$ (18)

and by symmetry,

$$n_H = n_F = \frac{\mu L}{F\sigma}.$$ (19)

Substituting (19) into (15), the price index becomes

$$G = \left(\frac{2L}{F\sigma}\right)^{\frac{1}{1-\sigma}} \frac{\sigma c}{\sigma - 1}.$$ (20)

Comparing (20) with (14), it can be confirmed that the price index is lower in the trading equilibrium than in autarky, because consumers now have access to the M goods both produced locally and abroad. This implies that welfare has improved due to the increased mass of the varieties of the M good available in the trading equilibrium than in the autarkic equilibrium.[ix]

Labor will be allocated to industries M and A, according to the expenditure share μ. That is, in each country μL workers are employed in the M industry and the remaining $(1-\mu)L$ workers are employed in the A industry.

Trading equilibrium with entry regulation

We finally consider the equilibrium when one country takes on a policy of regulating entry in the M good industry. Without loss of generality, it is assumed that the foreign country introduces a policy that restricts entry into the M sector. In contrast, there is no such regulation in the home country. Let us assume then that $n_F = xn_H$ where $0 < x < 1$. x is a policy variable that the foreign country sets.

Since free entry in the home country still prevails, there are no profits to be made in the home country. Therefore,

$$q_H = \frac{F(\sigma-1)}{c} \tag{21}$$

still holds, which, in equilibrium, is equal to demand for each variety $\mu p^{-\sigma} G^{\sigma-1}(Y_H + Y_F)$. This pins down the firm size globally: since each foreign M firm faces the same size of demand, market clearing in the M goods imply

$$q_H = \frac{F(\sigma-1)}{c} = \mu p^{-\sigma} G^{\sigma-1}(Y_H + Y_F). \tag{22}$$

Hence, the M firms cannot raise profits either in the foreign country. Zero profits in both countries imply that (16) also holds under entry regulation in the foreign country.

The factor market clearing condition is now

$$2L = (1+x)(n_H F + n_H c q_H) + (1-\mu)Y. \tag{23}$$

Substituting (16) and (21) into (23) and solving for the masses of the M firms in each country, we obtain

$$n_H = \frac{2\mu L}{(1+x)F\sigma} \tag{24}$$

and

$$n_F = \frac{2x\mu L}{(1+x)F\sigma}. \tag{25}$$

From (24) and (25), we see that (18) still holds, that is, the global mass of M firms remains unchanged. This implies that (20) also holds under entry regulation, meaning that the mass of the varieties of the M good available does not change. Therefore, economic welfare remains unchanged in both countries, despite the regulatory policy introduced in the foreign country.

In equilibrium all workers are employed in industries M or A in each country. In the home country labor employed in the M industry is $n_H(F + c q_H)$, and in the foreign country it is $xn_H(F + c q_H)$. Substituting (22) and (24), they are

36   Chapter 4

$$\frac{2\mu L}{1+x} \qquad (26)$$

in the home country, and

$$\frac{2x\mu L}{1+x} \qquad (27)$$

in the foreign country. Correspondingly, labor employed in the A industry in the home country is $L - n_H \left(F + cq_H \right)$ and in the foreign country it is $L - xn_H \left(F + cq_H \right)$. Substituting (22) and (24), labor employed in the A industry is

$$\frac{L\left(1+x-2\mu\right)}{1+x} \qquad (28)$$

in the home country, and

$$\frac{L\left(1+x-2x\mu\right)}{1+x} \qquad (29)$$

in the foreign country. The results from (26) to (29) imply that, with entry regulation in the M industry in the foreign country, in the home country the M industry expands while the A industry contracts. In contrast, in the foreign country the M industry contracts while the A industry expands. These are shown diagrammatically in Figures 4.1 and 4.2.

Inspecting (28) and (29), however, it is necessary that they are both positive. That is, $1+x-2\mu > 0$, or

$$x > 2\mu - 1. \qquad (30)$$

If this condition is satisfied then for any level of x, the endogenous variables in the trading equilibrium with entry regulation will be as summarized in Table 4.1. If condition (30) is not satisfied, as illustrated in Figure 4.3, the equilibrium will be a kind of a corner solution in which the home country specializes in the M industry and the foreign country specializes in the A industry.

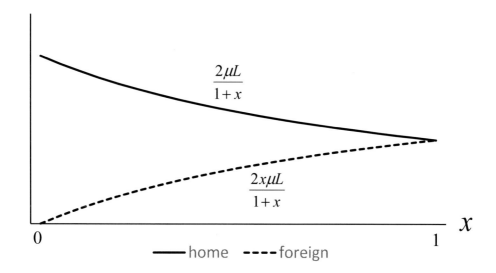

Figure 4.1: Labor allocated to the M industry

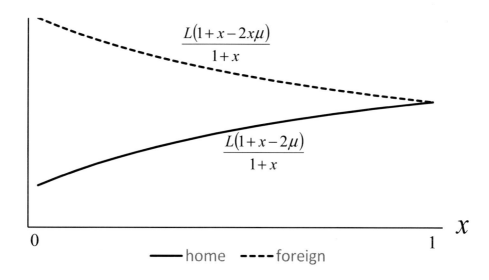

Figure 4.2: Labor allocated to the A industry

Table 4.1: Trading equilibrium with entry regulation

	Home	Foreign
M industry price index	\multicolumn{2}{c}{$G = \left(\dfrac{2L}{F\sigma}\right)^{\frac{1}{1-\sigma}} \dfrac{\sigma c}{\sigma-1}$}	
Firm mass in M industry	$n_H = \dfrac{2\mu L}{(1+x)F\sigma}$	$n_F = \dfrac{2x\mu L}{(1+x)F\sigma}$
Labor in M industry	$\dfrac{2\mu L}{1+x}$	$\dfrac{2x\mu L}{1+x}$
Labor in A industry	$\dfrac{L(1+x-2\mu)}{1+x}$	$\dfrac{L(1+x-2x\mu)}{1+x}$

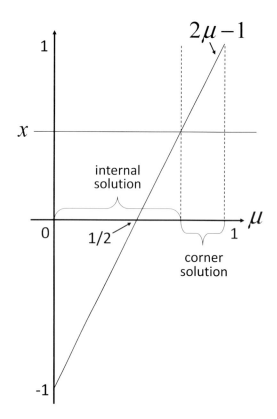

Figure 4.3: The non-specialization condition

5. Summary of Chapter 4

In this chapter the theoretical implications of a policy of entry regulation was studied under the free trade regime. The model used for the analysis was that of two symmetric countries with two industries. The firms in the M industry, which were producing differentiated goods, were monopolistically competitive and those in the A industry were perfectly competitive. Free trade was assumed in both industries.

Using the model, the consequences of the foreign country introducing a policy of regulating entry into the M industry was analyzed. It was found that when the mass of firms in the M industry in foreign is reduced by entry restriction, the same mass of firms enter in the home market to maintain the total mass of firms in the two countries. This implies that the policy does change the industrial composition within each country. That is, the home country tends to specialize in the M industry while the foreign country tends to specialize in the A industry.

From the consumers' point of view, even if an entry regulation policy is taken in one country, the world total mass of varieties of the M good available is maintained constant and does not change. In the foreign country, the loss in the mass of locally produced varieties is completely replaced by imported varieties from the home country. Therefore, competition policy of this kind introduced in one country does not affect the consumers in any country. In other words, in the country that regulates entry, free trade keeps the consumers from losing.

[ix] This is fundamentally the variety gains from trade set out by Krugman (1979, 1981).

Chapter 5 Natural advantage and economic geography: when does a mining site develop into a city?

1. Introduction

When does a mining site become a mining city? Mining sites are special locations that allow the accumulation and extraction of natural resources. Beyond this, when and why do such locations attract corporate activities leading to the creation of a city? Casual observation of geography illuminates examples of mining sites that have become cities, including Johannesburg in South Africa, Kalgoorlie in Australia, and Magnitogorsk in Russia. However, not all mining sites become cities, which suggests that either the subsequent development of mining sites into cities is a random phenomenon or that conditions exist under which those sites develop into cities.

Since Krugman (1991), the agglomeration of economic activities has been studied from the perspective of new economic geography. Krugman (1993) analyzed the location of a city that serves an agricultural hinterland by supplying manufactured goods. He established that a city can be formed in a location without significant natural advantages, or first nature, and that there are multiple equilibria for metropolitan location. Fujita et. al. (1999) studied how population increase leads to the evolution of a system of cities, based on the city and agricultural hinterland setting.

This study follows the literature defining cities as a concentration of manufacturing activities. In addition to a city, a special location is considered. Specifically, it is a mining site, which serves the city by supplying natural resources. Mining requires workers at the mining site. The workers in turn need consumption goods to survive and meet other well-being demands. From the mining site, natural resources are sent to the city, excepting the resources needed by the miners themselves to live. In the city, various varieties of goods are produced by industries other than mining. Miners consume goods produced in, and subsequently shipped in from, the city. All firms producing consumption goods operate in the city initially. But the firms are mobile and they are free to locate elsewhere. Under such circumstances, would the mining site ever become an attractive place for firms to relocate to? If so, then a new city may be created at the mining site. That is, the mining site becomes a mining city. This chapter analyzes under what conditions a mining site can develop into a city. Previewing the main finding, a range of potential locations of mining sites that can develop into a mining city is derived. A mining site outside this range will remain as a mining site.

After configuring the model in Section 2 and deriving the behavior of the salient economic agents in Section 3, the equilibrium of a city and a mining site is derived in

42 Chapter 5

Section 4. It is shown that city size and mining depend on the cost of trade between the city and the mining site, among other factors. Analysis of equilibrium stability identifies conditions for new city creation at the mining site.

2. Assumptions

There are two locations, the city and the mining site. There are two industries, manufacturing and mining. Manufacturing takes place in the city and mining takes place at the mining site. The total labor force is $\bar{L}$, and these workers are employed either by manufacturing firms or by mining firms. The workers are free to choose either occupation. A worker employed in manufacturing lives in the city. A worker employed in mining lives at a residential facility at the mining site. λ is the share of workers in mining, and correspondingly $1-\lambda$ is the share of manufacturing workers. So, given λ, the population of workers in the city is $(1-\lambda)\bar{L}$ and that in the mining site is $\lambda\bar{L}$.

In manufacturing, each firm produces its own variety of goods which are differentiated from the varieties produced by other firms. Manufacturing firms therefore compete in product differentiation and they are assumed to be monopolistically competitive. In the mining sector, each miner extracts a unit of the natural resource. The mining sector is assumed to be perfectly competitive.

Since manufacturing only exists in the city and mining only takes place at the mining site, the goods are shipped between the two locations: some of the manufactured goods are sent from the city to the mining site, and some of the resources extracted at the mining site are sent to the city. It is assumed that the natural resources do not require trade costs but the manufactured goods do. This assumption can be interpreted as follows. Although both natural resources and manufactured goods incur physical transportation costs, the former but not the latter are also associated with other costs, such as distribution costs. This assumption implies, in relative terms, that manufacturing trade costs are higher than those of natural resources.

The geographical set up presented above is also illustrated in Figure 5.1, and it implies that the city has advantages because prices are lower than at the mining site. To elaborate, prices, or living costs, are higher at the mining site because every manufactured good has to be transported from the existing city.

All members of the economy not only work but also consume. It is assumed that they have homogenous preferences described by the following two-tier structure:

$$U = M^{\mu}R^{1-\mu} \quad (0 < \mu < 1) \tag{1}$$

$$M = \left[\int_0^n m(i)^{\rho} \, di \right]^{\frac{1}{\rho}} \quad (0 < \rho < 1) \tag{2}$$

The upper tier (1) is a Cobb-Douglas function of the consumption of an aggregate of the varieties of the manufactured good (M) and the consumption of the natural resource (R). The second tier (2) defines M to be a CES (constant elasticity of substitution) function where $m(i)$ is the consumption of each variety i of the M good. M is therefore a CES composite of the total mass of varieties n. The elasticity of substitution between any manufactured varieties is $1/(1-\rho) \equiv \sigma$ ($\sigma > 1$).

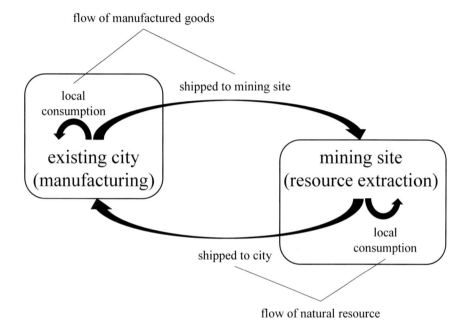

Figure 5.1: States and flows between the city and mining site

3. Consumer and firm behavior

Consumer behavior

Given income Y, price of natural resource p^R, and price of each M variety $p(i)$, the consumer's problem is to maximize her utility subject to the budget constraint

$$\int_0^n p(i)m(i)\,di + p^R R = Y. \qquad (3)$$

As derived in Chapter 1, the demand functions for manufactured variety j and the agricultural good, respectively, are

$$m(j) = p(j)^{-\sigma} G^{\sigma-1} \mu Y \qquad (4)$$

and

44   Chapter 5

$$R = \frac{(1-\mu)Y}{p^R},$$ (5)

respectively, where the price index G is

$$G \equiv \left[\int_0^n p(i)^{\frac{\rho}{\rho-1}} di\right]^{\frac{\rho-1}{\rho}} = \left[\int_0^n p(i)^{1-\sigma} di\right]^{\frac{1}{1-\sigma}}.$$ (6)

Firm behavior

Each firm in the manufacturing industry produces a particular variety of manufactured goods, but there is some degree of competition because other rival firms produce similar goods. A typical monopolistically competitive firm will set its price so that marginal revenue equals marginal cost (c). Then, denoting the unit price of the manufactured good in the existing city as p , and the manufacturing wage as w , we have

$$p(1-1/\sigma) = cw.$$ (7)

This is known as mark-up pricing, where firms always set their prices above their marginal costs. (Hereafter, i will be omitted to simplify the notation.) Since rival firms are producing more or less substitutable varieties, the mark-up depends on σ : when the varieties are close substitutes (or consumers do not exhibit strong preferences for variety), i.e., when σ is high, then consumers are sensitive to price and they come closer to c .

Substituting (7) into (6), we have the price index of the manufactured good in the city (Hereafter, subscript C denotes city):

$$G_C = \left(\frac{\sigma cw}{\sigma-1}\right) n^{\frac{1}{1-\sigma}}.$$ (8)

Given the 'iceberg' trade cost $t > 1$, the delivered price of the manufactured good at the mining site is pt , which is always higher than the price in the city. Therefore, introducing subscript M to denote 'mining site', the price index for manufactured goods at the mining site becomes

$$G_M = \left(\frac{\sigma cw}{\sigma-1}\right) tn^{\frac{1}{1-\sigma}}.$$ (9)

4. Equilibrium and its stability

The initial equilibrium

Equilibrium is defined as a situation in which, allowing free entry, the goods and factor markets clear. In addition, because workers are freely mobile between the city and the mining site, equilibrium requires that real wages are equalized in the two locations.

The profit of a typical manufacturing firm (π) is

$$\pi = pq - Fw - cqw. \tag{10}$$

Free entry, however, drives π down to zero. Substituting (7) into (10) and setting it equal to zero, we have

$$q = \frac{F(\sigma - 1)}{c}, \tag{11}$$

which is the equilibrium size of a typical manufacturing firm. The market clearing condition for the manufactured good is

$$q = \mu p^{-\sigma} G_C^{\sigma-1} Y_C + \mu (pt)^{-\sigma} G_M^{\sigma-1} Y_M t, \tag{12}$$

where Y_C is the total income of the city and Y_M is the total income of the mining site. Y_C is equal to the total wage incomes of the workers in the city, that is,

$$Y_C = (1 - \lambda)\bar{L}w, \tag{13}$$

and Y_M is equal to the total wage incomes of the miners at the mining site. Because miners' wages are set equal to one,

$$Y_M = \lambda \bar{L}. \tag{14}$$

The factor market clearing condition is

$$n(F + cq) = (1 - \lambda)\bar{L}. \tag{15}$$

Substituting the price indices in (8) and (9) and the incomes in (13) and (14) into (12), we have

$$q = \mu p^{-1} n^{-1} \bar{L} \left[(1 - \lambda)w + \lambda \right]. \tag{16}$$

The real wage equalization condition requires

$$\frac{w}{G_C^\mu} = \frac{1}{G_M^\mu}. \tag{17}$$

Substituting (8) and (9) into (17), and solving for w, we have

$$w = \frac{G_C^\mu}{G_M^\mu} = \frac{1}{t}. \tag{18}$$

Given that $t > 1$, (18) means that the nominal wage is always lower in the city. In other words, the equilibrium mining wage is always higher than the city wage to compensate for the higher living costs at the mining site.

Substituting (11), (15), and (18) into (16) and solving, the share of miners is found to be

$$\lambda = \frac{1 - \mu}{\mu(t - 1) + 1}. \tag{19}$$

Substituting (19) into (15) and solving, the mass of manufacturing firms is found to be

$$n = \frac{\bar{L}}{F\sigma} \left[\frac{\mu t}{\mu(t - 1) + 1} \right]. \tag{20}$$

Result (19) implies that λ, the (relative) size of the mining sector, depends on the

46   Chapter 5

share of consumers' expenditure on manufactured goods (μ) and the trade cost (t). Since

$$\frac{d\lambda}{d\mu} < 0, \tag{21}$$

consistent with intuition, as the expenditure share on manufacturing rises, the size of mining declines. Also, inspecting (19), since

$$\frac{d\lambda}{dt} < 0, \tag{22}$$

the higher the trade cost, the smaller the size of mining. This is because higher trade cost reduces the (nominal) wage in the city, as derived in (18), and renders manufacturing more profitable relative to mining. In fact, it is confirmed that the higher trade cost increases the mass of manufacturing firms because

$$\frac{dn}{dt} > 0. \tag{23}$$

Stability of the initial equilibrium

Next, we consider the stability of the initial equilibrium derived above. Would it ever be profitable for manufacturing firms to leave the city and relocate to the mining site? The initial equilibrium is not stable when manufacturing can profitably relocate from the city to the mining site. If this is case, the mining site becomes a mining city.

Any manufacturing firm can execute the following decision-making calculation. Denoting the hypothetical price and demand for a typical manufacturing firm if it relocated to the mining site as $\tilde{p}$ and $\tilde{q}$, respectively, and the corresponding hypothetical profit as $\tilde{\pi}$, relocating to the mining site is profitable if

$$\tilde{\pi} = \tilde{p}\tilde{q} - (F + c\tilde{q})wt > 0. \tag{24}$$

Note, in (24), that the costs also change, because the workers need to be paid at least wages t times higher than in the city to compensate for the higher prices at the mining site. If (24) is satisfied then the initial equilibrium in which all manufacturing firms agglomerate in the city becomes unstable. Since

$$\tilde{p}(1 - 1/\sigma) = cwt, \tag{25}$$

and from (18), $wt = 1$, (24) simplifies to

$$\tilde{\pi} = \frac{c}{\sigma - 1}\tilde{q} - F. \tag{26}$$

$\tilde{q}$ can be calculated as follows. When a manufacturing firm relocates to the mining site, it must ship some of the manufactured goods to the city, and the delivered price of its product is pt in the city. Therefore,

$$\tilde{q} = \mu(\tilde{p}t)^{-\sigma} G_C^{\sigma-1} Y_C t + \mu \tilde{p}^{-\sigma} G_M^{\sigma-1} Y_M. \tag{27}$$

Using the results from the initial equilibrium, substituting for G_C, G_M, Y_C, and Y_M in (27), and rearranging, we have

$$\tilde{q} = \tilde{p}^{-1} n^{-1} \overline{L} \left[(1-\lambda) w t^{1-\sigma} + \lambda t^{\sigma-1} \right]. \tag{28}$$

Substituting (28) into (26) gives

$$\tilde{\pi} = F \left(t^{-\sigma} + \frac{\lambda}{1-\lambda} t^{\sigma-1} - 1 \right). \tag{29}$$

Further, substituting for λ in (29) using (19), it becomes

$$\tilde{\pi} = F \left(t^{-\sigma} + \frac{1-\mu}{\mu t} t^{\sigma-1} - 1 \right). \tag{30}$$

Given that $F > 0$, the mining site will become a mining city if

$$t^{-\sigma} + \frac{1-\mu}{\mu} t^{\sigma-2} - 1 > 0, \tag{31}$$

that is, new city creation at the mining site depends on parameters μ, t, and σ. Rearranging (31), we finally obtain

$$\mu > \frac{t^{\sigma-2}}{1 - t^{-\sigma} + t^{\sigma-2}} \equiv \Omega, \tag{32}$$

which is the condition for mining city development.

Inspecting (32), it can immediately be observed that the higher the value of μ, the higher the possibility of the mining site being an attractive place for the relocation of manufacturing firms and thus the creation of a new city. This result can be explained as follows. Higher μ implies higher demand for manufactured goods and, correspondingly, larger size of the existing city. The larger the city, the more intense the competition between manufacturing firms in the city. This provides incentives for manufacturing firms to leave the city and relocate to the mining site.

However, because

$$\frac{\partial \Omega}{\partial t} = \frac{t^{1+2\sigma} \left[2 + t^\sigma (\sigma-2) - 2\sigma \right]}{\left(-t^2 + t^{2\sigma} + t^{2+\sigma} \right)^2} \tag{33}$$

and

$$\frac{\partial \Omega}{\partial \sigma} = \frac{t^{2+2\sigma} \left(t^\sigma - 2 \right) \log t}{\left(-t^2 + t^{2\sigma} + t^{2+\sigma} \right)^2}, \tag{34}$$

how t and σ influence new city creation is ambiguous. To elaborate, higher t implies higher prices of manufactured goods at the mining site, which attracts firms and supports new city creation. At the same time, however, higher t implies that supplying the city from the mining site is costly and disadvantageous, which discourages firms' relocation to the mining site and new city creation. Hence, the effect of t on new city

48   Chapter 5

creation is ambiguous. Also, σ works both ways with regard to new city creation. Higher σ implies more intense price competition for the manufacturing firms, which supports new city creation. But higher σ also implies that supplying the city from the mining site is more disadvantageous, discouraging firms' relocation to the mining site.

Because of the abovementioned ambiguity, numerical analyses are henceforth employed. A graph of the right-hand side of (32), denoted as Ω, is shown in Figure 5.2a. This figure is drawn with $\sigma=3$. In this case there is a range of t within which the mining site develops into a city. The range illustrated in the graph corresponds to $\mu=0.8$. This result means that neither a mining site close to the city nor a mining site too far away from the city becomes a city.

Figure 5.2b is another graph of Ω, constructed for $\sigma=1.5$. It shows that the mining site becomes a city provided t exceeds a certain level. That is, a mining site becomes a city as long as it is not too close to the city. In either case, a mining site too close to the city does not become a new city. This result can be interpreted as the existence of an 'agglomeration shadow.'

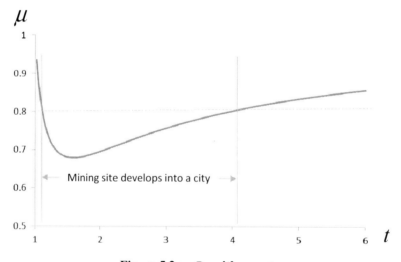

Figure 5.2a: Ω with $\sigma=3$

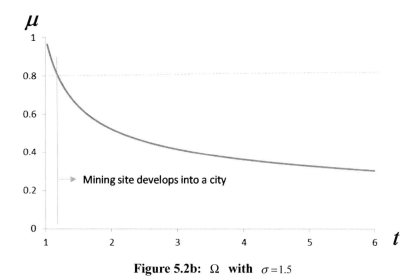

Figure 5.2b: Ω with $\sigma = 1.5$

5. Summary of Chapter 5

This study theoretically analyzed the equilibrium of a geographic setting comprising a city and a mining site. Analysis of the equilibrium showed that the sizes of the city and the mining site depend on trade costs between both places, among other factors. There is an inverse relationship between trade costs and size of the mining sector.

The conditions under which the mining site develops into another city were derived by analyzing the stability of the equilibrium. It was found that a higher expenditure share on manufactured goods, or industrialization of the economy, supports creation of a mining city. Numerical analyses suggest that there are ranges of trade costs between an existing city and a mining site that support mining city development, and that a lower degree of competition in the industrial sector supports development of mining sites into mining cities. These findings may help to explain why some mining sites become mining cities while others do not.

Chapter 6 Spatial organization of firms in a changing global economic environment: implications for Tokyo

1. Introduction

Metropolitan areas are important components of national economies today. According to the United Nations (2010), 48.6% of the world population live in cities, and in the developed economies of Europe, North America, Australia, New Zealand, and Japan, 73.9% of the population are urban dwellers. National economies, in turn, are not operating in isolation, but are interconnected with the rest of the global economy. The global economy is changing. In recent years, its growth center has undergone a clear shift. The so-called BRICs, China and India in particular, have risen as new economic superpowers. In addition, although multilateral talks in the WTO have halted, further international trade liberalization is on the way through numerous regional trade agreements. In the Asia-Pacific region, the economies are heading towards forming a large free trade area called the FTAAP, or Free Trade Area of Asia-Pacific. What, if any, are the implications of the changing global economic environment on metropolitan economies? This chapter aims to answer this question by analyzing a simple economic model of a metropolis in a global context and to provide implications for metropolitan economies such as Tokyo.

In today's economy, metropolitan economies are characterized by the service sector rather than by physical production in factories. One of the distinctive characteristics of the metropolitan service sector is the agglomeration of corporate headquarters (HQ). Major cities in the world today host corporate HQs, providing various producer services that the HQs need. As well documented by Sassen (2001), producer services and finance have grown very rapidly since the 1970s, and are highly concentrated in Tokyo in the case of Japan. The agglomeration of producer services attracts corporate HQs. In 2010, among the 71 Japanese companies listed in the Fortune Global 500, the HQs of 51 (71.8%) were located in Tokyo. This implies that the situation of a metropolis like Tokyo is closely related to the spatial organization of firms, that is, the way firms locate their various facilities and resources.

There are a number of existing empirical studies on the spatial organization of firms based on U.S. data. Davis and Henderson (2008) find that separating HQs from production sites leads to productivity advantages for firms. They emphasize the availability of differentiated local service input suppliers as a productivity advantage for firms that choose to locate their HQs in cities. At the same time, as Henderson and Ono (2008) investigated, there are trade-offs between the gains derived from separating the HQs from the production sites and the cost of communication and coordination between

52   Chapter 6

production and administration.

As will be revealed in Section 2, data from Japan indicate that firms with metropolitan HQs are larger than others, averaging about twice as large as those without metropolitan HQs. This fact suggests there being a productivity advantage in locating HQs in metropolitan areas, which supports Davis and Henderson's (2008) findings and suggests that, despite the cost associated with separating HQs as discussed in Henderson and Ono (2008), there is a net productivity advantage in deciding to split production and administration.

These empirical findings are the motivation behind our model of a metropolis that explains the coexistence of two types of firms: large productive firms with metropolitan stand-alone HQs and smaller firms with HQs and other facilities located together. The model incorporates a simple form of firm heterogeneity into a standard urban economy model in which residents commute to the HQs in the central business district (CBD). The firms are *ex ante* identical but deciding where to locate the firms' HQs creates an equilibrium outcome in which firms vary in size and productivity within the same industry. The model is extended to analyze potential links between the global economy and metropolitan areas through changes in the spatial organization of firms. The main finding of this analysis is that international trade liberalization is likely to promote concentration of HQs in the metropolitan areas. Greater international competition through trade liberalization can lead to a new equilibrium in which metropolitan areas grow larger to host more HQs and skilled workers, depending on the relative size of the economy. This result contrasts with findings by Krugman and Livas-Elizondo (1996) in the new economic geography literature, who present a theoretical hypothesis that trade liberalization reduces urban concentration, but provides support to the empirical finding by Nitsch (2006) that trade liberalization has promoted urban concentration in recent years.

Japan is facing two major changes in its global economic environment: one is that its economy is shrinking, partly due to a rapidly aging population that is also shrinking, and the other is globalization or increased competition through international trade liberalization. Japan's share of the world's economy has been on the decrease and is now less than 10% of the world GDP. Given that Japan's relative economic size is shrinking, further international trade liberalization is likely to spur further concentration in Tokyo, based on our model's predictions. This is because the advantages that locating HQs in Tokyo offers firms (in helping them to become productive and competitive and to gain in foreign markets) outweighs the cost of running HQs in Tokyo when their home economy is less important.

Globalization and Tokyo   53

The rest of the chapter is organized as follows. In the next section, findings from Japanese establishment and enterprise census data are presented to characterize the spatial organization of firms and the metropolis with which they relate in a modern industrialized economy. Based on the observations in Section 2, Section 3 presents an economic model of the spatial organization of firms with respect to a metropolis. Section 4 analyzes the impact of globalization. The final section presents our conclusions.

2. Spatial organization of firms and the metropolis – data from Japan

This section presents some characteristics of the current spatial organization of Japanese businesses. It is based on multi-unit firms, which employ around half of Japan's total corporate labor force. As shown in Table 6.1, nearly 70% of the firms have their HQs in major metropolitan areas, and these firms are twice as large as those without HQs in metropolitan areas.

Figures 6.1a and 6.1b plot the firm sizes and shares of employment in the prefectures where the HQs are located (as measures of the firms' spatial integration), respectively, against the population densities of the prefectures in which the HQs are located (as a measure of urbanization). Figure 6.1a suggests that firms with HQs in metropolitan areas tend to be larger. Figure 6.1b suggests that, in relative terms, firms with HQs in metropolitan areas are spatially dispersed, while firms with rural HQs are spatially integrated.

Figures 6.2a and 6.2b take closer looks by comparing firms with HQs in Tokyo (the capital and the biggest metropolis in Japan) to those with HQs in Kagoshima prefecture in southwestern Japan, which is relatively rural.[x] There is a stark difference between the two types. The regional employment distribution of the 'Tokyo firms' in Figure 6.2a suggests they are operating nationally, because only 25% of their employees are in Tokyo. (The bars in the figure add up to one.) In contrast, Figure 6.2b shows that the activities of the 'Kagoshima firms' are geographically concentrated within Kagoshima or neighboring prefectures, because more than 80% are employed locally.

Table 6.2 provides a breakdown by industry. The same trend as noted above appears in all industries except agriculture and mining. In those two, the majority of firms' HQs are in rural areas, and the differences in the sizes of firms with metropolitan and rural HQs are smaller. This may suggest that in these sectors, where products are less likely to be differentiated, locating HQs in metropolitan areas is less important.

The contrast between these two types of firms suggests that the HQ location does matter: there is indeed a net advantage in locating HQs in the metropolis as found by Davis and Henderson (2008), and the advantage allows firms with stand-alone

54   Chapter 6

metropolitan HQs to operate at much larger scales. Such large firms with spatially dispersed structures may be seen as 'national' firms. Smaller firms with their HQs and other facilities located close together in rural areas may be considered 'local' firms. A model that explains the coexistence of these two types of firms within the same industry and the corresponding size of the metropolis they are associated with as an equilibrium outcome is introduced in the next section.

Table 6.1: Spatial organization of firms in Japan

Location of HQs	Number of firms		Employment		Average firm size
Urban	138,535	69.1%	19,554,837	82.8%	141.2
Rural	61,926	30.9%	4,068,759	17.2%	65.7
Total	200,461	100.0%	23,623,596	100.0%	117.8

Note: "Urban" refers to firms with HQs in the 14 major metropolitan areas in Japan.

Source: Ministry of Internal Affairs and Communications (2006)

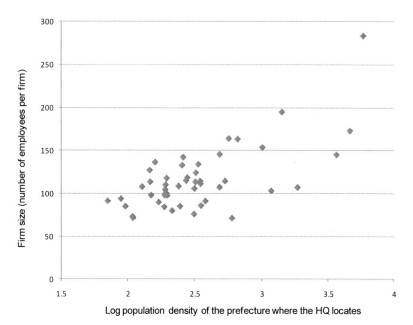

Source: Ministry of Internal Affairs and Communications (2006)

Figure 6.1a: HQ location and firm size

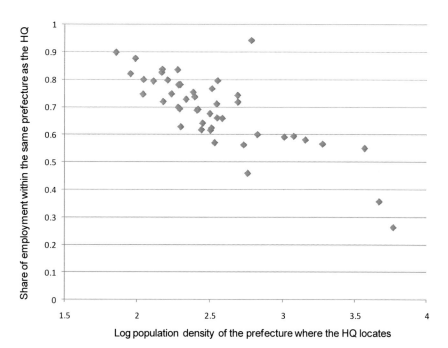

Source: Ministry of Internal Affairs and Communications (2006)

Figure 6.1b: HQ location and spatial organization of firms

56   Chapter 6

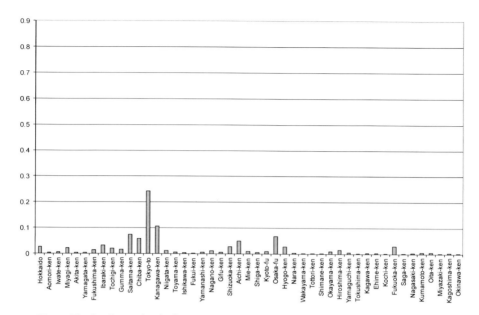

Note: The horizontal axis lists Japan's 47 prefectures.
Source: Ministry of Internal Affairs and Communications (2006)

Figure 6.2a: Geographic distribution of an average Tokyo firm's employment

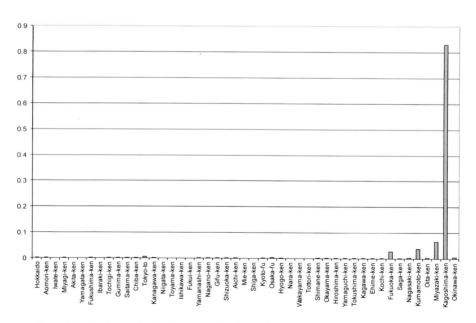

Note: The horizontal axis lists Japan's 47 prefectures.
Source: Ministry of Internal Affairs and Communications (2006)

Figure 6.2b: Geographic distribution of an average Kagoshima firm's employment

Globalization and Tokyo   57

Table 6.2: Spatial organization of firms by industry

	Location of HQs	Number of firms		Employment		Average firm size	urban/rural
All	Urban	138,535	69.1%	19,554,837	82.8%	141.2	2.15
	Rural	61,926	30.9%	4,068,759	17.2%	65.7	
	Total	200,461	100.0%	23,623,596	100.0%	117.8	
Agriculture, forestry and fishery	Urban	285	38.5%	16,462	41.5%	57.8	1.14
	Rural	456	61.5%	23,162	58.5%	50.8	
	Total	741	100.0%	39,624	100.0%	53.5	
Non-Agriculture	Urban	138,250	69.2%	19,538,375	82.8%	141.3	2.15
	Rural	61,470	30.8%	4,045,570	17.2%	65.8	
	Total	199,720	100.0%	23,583,945	100.0%	118.1	
Mining	Urban	115	38.9%	6,799	51.1%	59.1	1.65
	Rural	181	61.1%	6,497	48.9%	35.9	
	Total	296	100.0%	13,296	100.0%	44.9	
Construction	Urban	11,518	62.0%	960,023	75.5%	83.3	1.89
	Rural	7,051	38.0%	310,700	24.5%	44.1	
	Total	18,569	100.0%	1,270,723	100.0%	68.4	
Manufacturing	Urban	26,002	72.7%	4,873,757	83.0%	187.4	1.83
	Rural	9,765	27.3%	1,000,824	17.0%	102.5	
	Total	35,767	100.0%	5,874,581	100.0%	164.2	
Information and communication	Urban	3,767	81.4%	881,246	91.0%	233.9	2.32
	Rural	861	18.6%	86,956	9.0%	101.0	
	Total	4,628	100.0%	968,202	100.0%	209.2	
Transportation	Urban	6,487	69.9%	1,418,248	82.7%	218.6	2.06
	Rural	2,793	30.1%	296,069	17.3%	106.0	
	Total	9,280	100.0%	1,714,317	100.0%	184.7	
Wholesale and retail	Urban	51,871	66.9%	5,327,742	79.9%	102.7	1.97
	Rural	25,718	33.1%	1,338,759	20.1%	52.1	
	Total	77,589	100.0%	6,666,501	100.0%	85.9	
Finance and insurance	Urban	1,236	72.7%	870,442	88.2%	704.2	2.81
	Rural	464	27.3%	116,340	11.8%	250.7	
	Total	1,700	100.0%	986,782	100.0%	580.5	
Real estate	Urban	5,275	82.0%	327,925	91.4%	62.2	2.34
	Rural	1,157	18.0%	30,674	8.6%	26.5	
	Total	6,432	100.0%	358,599	100.0%	55.8	
Restaurant and hotel	Urban	7,819	65.9%	1,391,794	83.6%	178.0	2.65
	Rural	4,050	34.1%	272,091	16.4%	67.2	
	Total	11,869	100.0%	1,663,885	100.0%	140.2	
Medical and welfare	Urban	1,566	76.1%	154,264	86.7%	98.5	2.06
	Rural	493	23.9%	23,622	13.3%	47.9	
	Total	2,059	100.0%	177,886	100.0%	86.4	
Education	Urban	2,040	74.2%	262,786	88.3%	128.8	2.62
	Rural	709	25.8%	34,878	11.7%	49.2	
	Total	2,749	100.0%	297,664	100.0%	108.3	
Other service	Urban	20,420	71.4%	2,904,004	85.0%	142.2	2.27
	Rural	8,162	28.6%	510,486	15.0%	62.5	
	Total	28,582	100.0%	3,414,490	100.0%	119.5	

Source: Ministry of Internal Affairs and Communications (2006).

3. Model of the spatial organization of firms and the metropolis

This section introduces a model of the spatial organization of firms focusing on their choice of corporate HQ location and the mobility of skilled workers working for the firms, who form the metropolis.

3.1. Assumptions

Goods, production technology, and market structure

There are two types of goods in the economy: differentiated and homogeneous. Differentiated goods are produced by manufacturing firms. A manufacturing firm's facilities consist of a HQ and a factory. The HQ manages the factory, and producer services are essential for the HQ to operate and make decisions. There are two types of workers in the economy: skilled and unskilled. The HQ requires a fixed number (F) of skilled workers, and factory production requires a fixed number (m) of unskilled workers per unit output. Manufacturing firms thus face increasing returns to scale. The total cost of producing a given amount q is

$$C(q) = Fw^S + mqw^U \tag{1}$$

where w^S and w^U are the wages of skilled and unskilled workers, respectively. Manufacturing firms are assumed to be monopolistically competitive: each firm competes with others by producing a variety of differentiated goods.

The homogeneous good is produced using unskilled workers only, under constant-returns-to-scale technology and perfect competition. Consumers have positive initial endowments of the homogeneous good ($\bar{q}_0$) and it is chosen as the numeraire good. The homogeneous good, therefore, is a basic measurement unit. Assuming that a unit of unskilled worker produces a unit of the homogeneous good, we have $w^U = 1$ in equilibrium.

Spatial organization of firms and the metropolis

The metropolis is defined as a location that provides producer services to corporate HQs. Examples of producer services include financial services, legal services, consultations, marketing, etc.[xi] The manufacturing firms purchase producer services through their HQs. Firms can separate their HQs and locate them as stand-alone facilities in the metropolis. This is beneficial because the location of the HQ affects factories' productivity. Specifically, due to their proximity to producer services, manufacturing firms with stand-alone metropolitan HQs obtain net productivity advantages. Such firms will be called 'separated' firms hereafter. Their cost function is

$$C(q^{SEP}) = Fw_M^S + Amq^{SEP}w^U, \tag{2a}$$

where $0 < A < 1$, and subscript M and superscript SEP stand for metropolis and separated, respectively. Coefficient A represents the net productivity advantage that the firm gains from having its HQ in the metropolis. The smaller the value of A, the larger the productivity advantage. In contrast, firms whose HQs are not in the metropolis face higher marginal costs because their HQs lack face-to-face communication with the producer service providers and hence have poorer access to those producer services. These firms will be called 'integrated' firms hereafter. They employ skilled workers for their HQs and unskilled workers for their factories in rural areas. The total cost for an integrated firm is

$$C\left(q^{INT}\right) = Fw_R^S + mq^{INT}w^U, \tag{2b}$$

where R and INT stand for rural and integrated, respectively.

As in standard models of urban economics, the metropolis has the following internal geographic structure: metropolitan HQs are located in the center of the metropolis, the CBD, where producer services are available. This implies that those living in the metropolis must commute to the CBD from their residences. We assume that the CBD itself is dimensionless and that a fixed lot of land is necessary for each individual's dwelling place in the metropolis.[xii]

The metropolitan population consists of skilled workers who are working in the metropolitan HQs. The rural population consists of skilled workers working in the rural HQs of the integrated firms, and unskilled workers employed in their manufacturing factories or in the homogeneous good sector. Skilled workers can move between the metropolis and rural areas, and those who work in metropolitan HQs can live anywhere in the metropolis. The share of skilled workers in the metropolis is λ. Correspondingly, the share of skilled workers working in rural HQs is $1 - \lambda$.

Consumer preference
As is the case with many economic models, consumer behavior must be specified in order to derive an expression for the demand for the variety of manufactured goods that each firm produces. Consumer preference and the corresponding demand structure follows Ottaviano et al. (2002).[xiii] All consumers have the same preferences with the following utility function:

$$U = \alpha \int_{i=0}^{n} c_i di - \frac{\beta - \delta}{2} \int_{i=0}^{n} c_i^2 di - \frac{\delta}{2} \left(\int_{i=0}^{n} c_i di \right)^2 + c^A \ (0 < \alpha, 0 < \delta < \beta), \tag{3}$$

where c_i is consumption of variety i of the manufactured good, c^A is consumption of the homogeneous good, and n is the total mass of varieties/firms producing the

60   Chapter 6

manufactured goods. α, β, and γ are exogenous parameters. α represents the intensity of the preferences for the manufactured good, and $\beta > \delta$ is required for the utility function to exhibit a love-of-variety. For a given value of β, δ expresses the substitutability between the varieties. Expression (3) appears to be complex, but as shown below in expression (5), its advantage is that it leads to a handy demand expression. With the budget constraint

$$\int_{i=0}^{n} p_i q_i di + q_0 = w + \overline{q}_0 , \tag{4}$$

which simply states that consumption of manufactured and homogeneous goods (left-hand side) is constrained by one's wage and initial endowment (right-hand side). Consumers' utility maximization behavior yields the following linear demand function for a typical variety of the manufactured good:

$$c_i = a - (b + cn) p_i + cP , \tag{5}$$

where p_i is the price of variety i and

$$a \equiv \frac{\alpha}{\beta + \delta(n-1)} , \quad b \equiv \frac{a}{\alpha} , \quad c \equiv \frac{\delta b}{\beta - \delta} , \quad P \equiv \int_{i=0}^{n} p_i di .$$

Expression (5) means that demand from each consumer for each firm (c_i) depends not only on the price (p_i) that the firm sets on its product but also on the overall price level (P). Of course, as p_i rises, c_i drops, and as P rises, c_i increases, other things being equal. Therefore, consistent with intuition, firms that can set their prices low relative to the overall price level in the industry will have larger demand than others who cannot.

3.2. Firm behavior

As is common with most economic models, we assume that firms are profit-maximizing entities. Given (5), the profit of a typical separated firm can be written as

$$\left(p^{SEP} - Am \right) \left[a - (b + cn) p^{SEP} + cP \right] (S + L) - Fw_M^S , \tag{6}$$

where S and L are the total numbers of skilled and unskilled workers (who are also consumers), respectively. Expression (6) simply means that each firms' profit is equal to per unit profit ($p^{SEP} - Am$) times demand from each consumer $[a - (b + cn) p^{SEP} + cP]$ times population ($S + L$) minus the fixed cost, which is the wages paid to its skilled workers (Fw_M^S). To maximize its profit (6), the separated firm will set its price at

$$p^{SEP} = \frac{1}{2} \left(Am + \frac{a + cP}{b + cn} \right) \tag{7a}$$

Technically, this is obtained by differentiating (6) with respect to p^{SEP} and setting it equal to zero. Similarly, the profit-maximizing price for an integrated firm can be obtained as

$$p^{INT} = \frac{1}{2}\left(m + \frac{a+cP}{b+cn}\right).$$ (7b)

(7a) and (7b) together imply a constant price differential of

$$p^{SEP} - p^{INT} = \frac{m(A-1)}{2} < 0$$ (8)

between the varieties produced by the separated and the integrated firms. That is, the separated firms always set lower prices than the integrated firms. How can integrated firms survive with their prices being higher than those of separated firms? This is because of consumers' preference for variety. They allocate their expenditures to all the available varieties, including the expensive ones produced by the integrated firms. Under such circumstances, integrated firms, even with their higher marginal costs and prices, can still exist. The size, i.e., per-firm output of each integrated firm will be smaller than those of separated firms, however, as will be shown below.

3.3. Spatial organization of firms and the equilibrium size of the metropolis

Equilibrium is defined as a situation in which all goods and labor markets clear, firms earn zero (pure) profits due to free entry, and the mobile skilled workers in the metropolis and in rural areas achieve the same utility level.

Market clearing of the manufactured goods requires

$$q^{SEP} = \left[a - (b+cn)p^{SEP} + cP\right](S+L),$$ (9a)

and

$$q^{INT} = \left[a - (b+cn)p^{INT} + cP\right](S+L).$$ (9b)

(9a) and (9b) state that the supply of manufactured goods (left-hand side) equals demand (right-hand side) for both separated and integrated firms. (9a) and (9b) together imply a constant size differential between the separated and the integrated firms:

$$q^{SEP} - q^{INT} = \frac{1-A}{2}m(b+cn)(S+L) > 0,$$ (10)

that is, separated firms always operate at larger scales. Given that the separated firms' functions are spatially dispersed between the metropolis and the rural area, and that they are bigger, separated firms come to operate on a national basis (like the 'Tokyo firms' in Section 2). Integrated firms, on the other hand, operate within smaller geographic areas and on smaller scales, so they act as local firms (like the 'Kagoshima firms' in Section 2).

Assuming free entry and exit, profits are driven to zero. Equilibrium skilled wages are then derived as

62 Chapter 6

$$w_M^S = \frac{1}{4F}\left(\frac{a+cP}{b+cn} - Am\right)\left[2a - Am(b+cn) + 2cP\right](S+L),$$ (11a)

and

$$w_R^S = \frac{1}{4F}\left(\frac{a+cP}{b+cn} - m\right)\left[2a - m(b+cn) + 2cP\right](S+L).$$ (11b)

As shown in Figure 6.3, if R is the land rent in the CBD, θ is the commuting cost per unit distance, and X is the distance from the CBD to the outer edge of the metropolis, then the disposable income of the skilled worker living closest to the CBD is $w_M^S - R$; he has no commuting cost but pays the highest rent (R). At the other extreme, the disposable income of the skilled worker living at the outer edge of the metropolis is $w_M^S - \theta X$; he pays no land rent but has the highest commuting cost (θX). Since all skilled workers are mobile within the metropolis, all residents earn the same disposable income, that is, $w_M^S - R = w_M^S - \theta X$ holds. Further, since full employment of skilled workers implies

$$n^{SEP} = \frac{\lambda S}{F} \quad \text{and} \quad n^{INT} = \frac{(1-\lambda)S}{F},$$ (12)

the metropolitan population $n^{SEP}F$ is equal to λS. The unit land requirement for each metropolitan resident implies $X = n^{SEP}F$. Therefore, in equilibrium,

$$R = \theta X = \theta\lambda S.$$ (13)

The total land rent is $RX/2 = \theta(\lambda S)^2/2$, and to simplify the analysis by abstracting away from explicitly modeling landowners, the land is assumed to be equally distributed between the metropolitan residents. Since the metropolitan population is λS, each receives $\theta\lambda S/2$ of it. The net urban cost for each individual is therefore $\theta\lambda S - \theta\lambda S/2$, that is, $\theta\lambda S/2$. In addition, skilled workers' free mobility requires that their utilities in the metropolis and in the rural area be equal. That is,

$$w_M^S - \frac{\theta\lambda S}{2} = w_R^S.$$ (14)

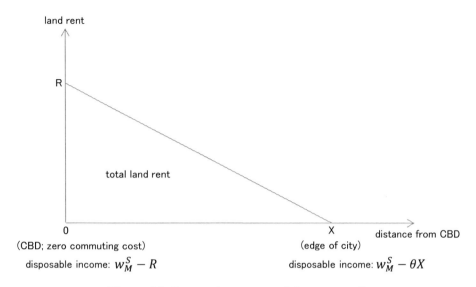

Figure 6.3: Internal structure of the metropolis

Because of the obvious productivity advantage of the separated/national firms, nominal skilled wages are higher in the metropolis. However, sufficiently high urban costs of land rent and commuting can lead to an equilibrium in which not all skilled workers work and reside in the metropolis. Figure 6.4 shows metropolitan and rural skilled wages as a function of the share of skilled workers in the metropolis, λ. The two wage curves, w_M^S and w_R^S, are downward sloping. This is because competition gets 'tougher', i.e., the average price level (P) declines as more firms locate their HQs in the metropolis and become productive. As shown in (14), the equilibrium distribution of skilled workers (λ) and the corresponding metropolis size are determined at the intersection of the $w_M^S - \theta\lambda S/2$ and w_R^S curves.[xiv] Inspecting (11a) and (11b) confirms that

$$\frac{\partial w_M^S}{\partial \lambda} - \frac{\partial w_R^S}{\partial \lambda} = -\frac{(A-1)^2 cm^2 S(L+S)(bF+cS)}{2F^2(2bF+cS)} < 0, \quad (15)$$

and so a stable internal solution ($0 < \lambda < 1$) can exist. Otherwise, all HQs and all skilled workers would choose to locate in the metropolis ($\lambda = 1$).

64   Chapter 6

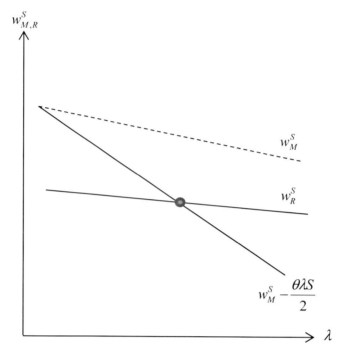

Figure 6.4: Equilibrium metropolis size

The above analysis can be summarized by the following point:

Result 1. There is an equilibrium in which two types of firms within the same industry coexist – spatially dispersed large firms with metropolitan HQs (separated/national firms) and spatially integrated smaller firms not located in the metropolis (integrated/local firms).

4. Spatial organization of firms and the metropolis in the global economy

Next, the external economy is introduced into the model to investigate its potential impact on the spatial organization of firms within the economy and on the metropolis.

4.1. Firm behavior abroad

Firms can now sell their products not only at home but also in foreign markets through exports. We assume that international trade costs τ units of the numeraire per unit of manufactured goods, and for simplicity, the numeraire good does not require trade costs. The profits of domestic separated and integrated firms' profits from foreign markets are then

$$\left(p_f^{SEP} - Am - \tau\right)\left[a - \left(b + cn^W\right)p_f^{SEP} + cP_f\right]\left(S_f + L_f\right), \tag{16a}$$

and

$$\left(p_f^{INT} - m - \tau\right)\left[a - \left(b + cn^W\right)p_f^{INT} + cP_f\right]\left(S_f + L_f\right), \tag{16b}$$

respectively, where f stands for foreign and n^W denotes the total mass of firms in the world. There are competitors in the foreign market. Foreign firms' profit in the foreign market is

$$\left(p_f^f - m^f\right)\left[a - \left(b + cn^W\right)p_f^f + cP_f\right]\left(S_f + L_f\right). \tag{16c}$$

Firms' profit maximization results in pricing behavior as summarized in Table 6.3, where h denotes home, p_f is the local price set by foreign manufacturing firms in the foreign market, and $m^f > 0$ is the foreign firms' productivity parameter. Hereafter, to focus on the impact of international competition, international trade costs are assumed not to be prohibitively high.

Table 6.3: Pricing behavior

	Home market	Foreign market
Home SEP (national) firms	$p_h^{SEP} = \dfrac{1}{2}\left(Am + \dfrac{a + cP_h}{b + cn^W}\right)$	$p_f^{SEP} = p_f^f + \dfrac{1}{2}\left(Am - m^f + \tau\right)$
Home INT (local) firms	$p_h^{INT} = \dfrac{1}{2}\left(m + \dfrac{a + cP_h}{b + cn^W}\right)$	$p_f^{INT} = p_f^f + \dfrac{1}{2}\left(m - m^f + \tau\right)$
Foreign firms	$p_h^f = \dfrac{a + cP_h + \left(m^f + \tau\right)\left(b + cn^W\right)}{2\left(b + cn^W\right)}$	$p_f^f = \dfrac{1}{2}\left(m^f + \dfrac{a + cP_f}{b + cn^W}\right)$

4.2. Trade equilibrium

The trade equilibrium is obtained by simultaneously solving the modified goods market clearing conditions derived from (9a) and (9b) by adding demands from the foreign market, the modified labor market clearing conditions using (12), and the zero profit conditions using (16a), (16b), and (16c).

4.3. Trade liberalization and the metropolis – the impact of trade liberalization (lower τ)

Improved access to the foreign market through a lower τ leads to increased output or firm size, which, in turn raises the operating profits and correspondingly wages of skilled

66   Chapter 6

workers in both separated/national and integrated/local firms, w_M^S and w_R^S, respectively. In addition, because the operating profits from abroad for the separated/national firms are higher due to their productivity advantage, the wages for skilled workers (w_M^S) can increase more. This is shown in Figure 6.5 as an unequal upward shift of the w_M^S and the w_R^S curves. Despite the urban costs, the relative increase in w_M^S induces skilled workers and HQs of integrated/local firms to relocate to the metropolis, until the increased urban costs put a brake on it.

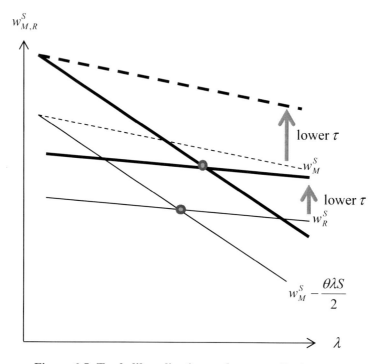

Figure 6.5: Trade liberalization and metropolis size

However, a reduction in international trade costs can negatively affect skilled wages as well. This is because improved access to foreign markets not only leads to higher operating profits abroad for home firms, but also leads to increased import competition from foreign firms in the home market. Whether reducing international trade costs increases or decreases domestic skilled wages depends on country size: if the home economy is sufficiently large compared to the foreign economy, reduced trade costs could lead to lower skilled wages at home. The condition for this to happen is

$$\frac{L_f + S_f}{L + S} < \frac{cn_f}{2b + cn_f} < 1, \tag{17}$$

and the skilled wages of separated/national firms drop more:

$$\frac{\partial w_M^S}{\partial \tau} < \frac{\partial w_R^S}{\partial \tau} < 0 \,. \tag{18}$$

Therefore, in this case reduced international trade costs lead to a smaller metropolis. On the other hand, if the home economy is sufficiently small compared to the external economy, reduced international trade costs increase the metropolis size, as in Figure 6.5. The result that the metropolis becomes larger means that there are now more separated/national firms, which are more productive and larger than integrated/local firms. Therefore, trade liberalization also leads to an increase in average industrial productivity.

The analysis in this section can be summarized as follows:

Result 2. Unless (17) is satisfied, that is, as long as the home economy is sufficiently small compared to the foreign economy, reducing international trade cost increases the equilibrium metropolis size.

5. Summary of Chapter 6

By constructing and analyzing a simple economic model of a metropolis in which businesses decide to locate their headquarters in the city or in a rural area and assuming that skilled workers are mobile, this study showed that when the relative size of the home economy is sufficiently small, reducing international trade costs increases the equilibrium metropolis size. This analysis is relevant to the current situation of Japan and its capital, Tokyo.

The city of Tokyo alone has a population of 12 million and more than a quarter of the entire population of Japan resides in the greater Tokyo area. Such a concentration of resources and economic activities in Tokyo has long been subject to policy debates. Given the ongoing trend of international trade liberalization in the Asia-Pacific region and Japan's shrinking economy, our analysis suggests that the combined effect of these is likely to induce further concentration in Tokyo. If such is the case, since Tokyo has been and will be hit by natural disasters, most notably earthquakes, the issue of economic concentration in Tokyo may require further policy consideration from a risk and national security point of view.

Economic models are simplifications of the complex real world, focusing on only a few of the many aspects that could matter. One limitation of the present analysis is that it only points out one of the many potential impacts of globalization. The geographic setup of the model was simplified to just two locations: metropolitan and rural areas. The result, therefore, cannot be directly applied to countries with multi-polar metropolitan structures.

68　Chapter 6

---

[x] Population densities of Tokyo and Kagoshima are 11,526 per sq. km and 5,344 per sq. km, respectively.

[xi] In the case of Tokyo, it may also include central government offices. See for example, Sassen (2001, p.108).

[xii] For simplicity, outside the metropolis, the opportunity cost of land is assumed to be zero.

[xiii] This linear form is chosen for better analytical tractability. Qualitatively the same results are obtained using the constant elasticity of substitution (CES) demand structure.

[xiv] The analytical solution of λ is

$$\lambda = \frac{\dfrac{S+L}{4F}(1-A)m\left\{2a - m(1+A)\left(b+\dfrac{cS}{F}\right) + \dfrac{2cS}{F(2bF+cS)}\left[(bF+cS)m+Fa\right]\right\}}{S\left[t + \dfrac{S+L}{4F^2}(1-A)^2 cm^2\left(\dfrac{cS}{2bF+cS}+1\right)\right]}.$$

References

Baldwin, Richard, Rikard Forslid, Philippe Martin, Gianmarco Ottaviano, and Frederic Robert-Nicoud. 2003. *Economic Geography and Public Policy*. Princeton and Oxford: Princeton University Press.

Broda, Christian, and David E. Weinstein. 2006. "Globalization and the gains from variety" *Quarterly Journal of Economics* **121**, 541-585.

Carlsson, Bo. 1984. "The development and use of machine tools in historical perspective" *Journal of Economic Behavior & Organization* **5**, 91-114.

Davis, James C., and J. Vernon Henderson. 2008. "Agglomeration of headquarters" *Regional Science and Urban Economics* **38**, 445-460.

Deaton, Angus, and John Muellbauer. 1980. *Economics and Consumer Behavior*. Cambridge, New York: Cambridge University Press.

Dixit, Avinash K., and Joseph E. Stiglitz. 1977. "Monopolistic competition and optimum product diversity" *American Economic Review* **67**, 297-308.

Duguay, Claude R., Sylvain Landry, and Federico Pasin. 1997. "From mass production to flexible/agile production" *International Journal of Operations & Production Management* **17**, 1183-1195.

Forslid, Rikard, and Gianmarco I.P. Ottaviano. 2003. "An analytically solvable core-periphery model" *Journal of Economic Geography* **3**, 229-240.

Freeman, Chris, and Luc Soete. 1997. *The Economics of Industrial Innovation*. 3rd ed. Cambridge: MIT Press.

Fujita, Masahisa, Paul Krugman, and Tomoya Mori. 1999. "On the evolution of hierarchical urban systems" *European Economic Review* **43**, 209-251.

Global Entrepreneurship Monitor (GEM). 2014. *Global Report 2014*.

Henderson, J. Vernon, and Yukako Ono. 2008. "Where do manufacturing firms locate their headquarters?" *Journal of Urban Economics* **63**, 431-450.

Hounshell, David A. 1984. *From the American System to Mass Production, 1800-1932: The Development of Manufacturing Technology in the United States*. Baltimore: Johns Hopkins University Press.

Kenney, Martin, and Richard Florida. 1988. "Beyond Mass Production: Production and the Labor Process in Japan" *Politics & Society* **16**, 121-158.

Krugman, Paul R. 1979. "Increasing returns, monopolistic competition, and international trade" *Journal of International Economics* **9**, 469-479.

Krugman, Paul R. 1981. "Intraindustry Specialization and the Gains from Trade" *Journal of Political Economy* **89**, 959-973.

Krugman, Paul. 1991. "Increasing Returns and Economic Geography" *Journal of*

Political Economy **99**, 483-499.

Krugman, Paul. 1993. "First nature, second nature, and metropolitan location" *Journal of Regional Science* **33**, 129-144.

Krugman, Paul, and Raul Livas-Elizondo. 1996. "Trade policy and the Third World metropolis" *Journal of Development Economics* **49**, 137-150.

Ministry of Internal Affairs and Communications. 2006. *Establishment and Enterprise Census of Japan.*

Nitsch, Volker. 2006. "Trade Openness and Urban Concentration: New Evidence" *Journal of Economic Integration* **21**, 340-362.

Ottaviano, Gianmarco, Takatoshi Tabuchi, and Jacques-François Thisse. 2002. "Agglomeration and trade revisited" *International Economic Review* **43**, 409-435.

Pine, B. Joseph. 1993. *Mass Customization: The New Frontier in Business Competition.* Boston: Harvard Business School Press.

Sabel, Charles, and Jonathan Zeitlin. 1985. "Historical alternatives to mass production: politics, markets and technology in nineteenth-century industrialization" *Past and Present* **108**, 133-176.

Sassen, Saskia. 2001. *The Global City: New York, London, Tokyo.* 2nd Ed. Princeton: Princeton University Press.

United Nations. 2010. *World Urbanization Prospects*, 2009 revision.

Womack, James. P., Daniel T. Jones, and Daniel Roos. 1990. *The Machine that Changed the World.* New York: Macmillan.